KANTARA

A Novel

BY FOUAD BISHAY MICHAEL

CONTENTS

AL LODD

The land that's supposed to flow with milk and honey, as described by a mighty god, has been flowing with nothing but blood and tears, as had happened in the biblical narrative and, more certainly, during the Roman invasion, the Islamic conquest, and the subsequent Crusades. In those times, the weapons used were the words of a god and the swords of his prophets and followers, and the battlefields were confined to the neighboring countries of the Middle East, the limited area of the known world at the time. By the twentieth century, wars would have reached a new level of brutality. The modern armaments became efficient killing machines with the unprecedented explosive power of weapons of mass destruction in the hands of new prophets, who came from a different continent, brandishing a mandate from no god but their own impudent authority.

While the Ottoman Empire, which had dominated the Middle East for centuries, was gradually collapsing, an industrial revolution was taking hold in the northern countries, accompanied by a brew of new ideas, new philosophies, and new ideologies that led to two world wars but failed to bring peace to the land of the milk and honey. Besides destroying a European supremacist, fascist regime, they succeeded in dismantling the Ottoman Empire and expanding different ones. In the process, millions of people perished in the battlefields, in the cities, and in concentration camps. The victorious divided the spoils— Great Britain got the lion's share of the Middle Eastern countries, and France got the rest. In the meantime, a much more powerful empire was rising across the ocean to claim the twentieth century as its own and call it "The American Century."

In the middle of that century, or more precisely on January 10, 1948, a British officer rushed into the stationmaster's office at the Al Lodd Train Station.

"Hold the train. Don't let it leave the station," the British officer shouted in apparent urgency.

The stationmaster came from behind his desk and stood across from the officer. "What's going on?" He asked in a bewildered voice.

"Just make sure that the train doesn't leave the station. I'll explain everything later," the officer said. Then he reached for the telephone. "Connect me to the military headquarters," he said into the mouthpiece, as he motioned for the stationmaster to follow his orders.

The stationmaster judged that something terribly wrong must have happened. His standing orders were always to keep the trains on time as much as possible. Despite his curiosity, he decided not to question the British officer any further. He went out of the office and walked the length of the platform to where the locomotive's engineer was waiting for the signal to start his journey to Egypt. He explained his new orders to the engineer and then hurriedly returned to his office. The British officer was sitting behind the desk, still talking in the telephone.

The stationmaster's office was a large room in the southern end of a long building that occupied the southern third of the main passenger platform. More offices and storage rooms comprised the rest of the building. A wide passageway extended on each side of it and opened northward onto the rest of the platform. The office was sparsely furnished with a mahogany desk, opposite the back wall, and two dark wooden benches, one on each side of it. A door opened to the middle of the platform, and a large window was centered in each of the opposing walls. Through one of those windows, one could see the train in question and a score of British soldiers going in and out of its cars. The air smelled of dust mixed with the scents of hay and smoke and steam characteristic of the locomotive-train stations of that period.

A twelve year-old boy sat on one of the benches. Dressed in long, well-ironed trousers, a long-sleeved shirt with a starched collar, and black polished shoes, he appeared to be older than he actually was. His eyes reflected an inquisitive mind and a keen interest in what was going on around him. He was so completely absorbed in his own thoughts that he didn't initially respond when his name was called.

"David, my son." It was the stationmaster who said those words and then repeated them as he was directly facing his son and getting his attention.

"Listen, David," his father continued, "it will be a while before this train leaves. I'll keep your luggage here. Go back home, and I'll send someone to get you when the train is allowed to depart."

Reluctantly, David left his father's office and started his leisurely walk to the house.

The town of Al Lodd was a small settlement in the center of Palestine, midway between Yafa and Jerusalem. The British authorities, which ruled that country under a United Nations mandate, used it as a strategic hub with all the facilities needed for the care of their troops and employees and also to service the rail traffic that stretched along the Eastern Mediterranean.

The train station itself was a sprawling complex that spread around three passenger platforms, including the main one with the long building. A large repair depot for the locomotive engines and spacious storage-warehouses stood far off to one side. Extensive rail networks extended from the station in all major directions: north to Haifa and up farther to Lebanon and Syria; south to Gaza and then across the Sinai Desert and the Suez Canal to Cairo, Egypt; west to Yafa and Tel Aviv on the Mediterranean coast; and east to Jerusalem, Jordan, and Iraq.

A large British military base occupied the northwestern side of town, and a bustling city, Al Ramlah, was within a walking distance on its eastern side. A single paved road traversed the center of town, where stonewalled, single-family homes were aligned for a few blocks on each side of wide, tree-lined streets. Most of those homes consisted of two attached dwellings surrounded on all sides by small, well-kept gardens and enclosed by high, wire-linked fences. Branches of climbing rosebushes found their way up wire lattices, spreading abundant clusters of pink and red roses during the flowering season, as if to celebrate the generosity of that land and its sunny weather. A few separate, large villas, reserved for the British managers and a few of the elite Arabic employees, were built on strategic lots with more distinctive gardens and fences. A one-room school building—where young children were taught reading, writing, and basic math—was located at the edge of town next to a large football field. A convenience store was stocked with the basic daily needs of the locals; other major supplies were only available in the city of Al Ramlah, a few kilometers away. Walking was the only way to go around the town or to the train station; there were no private cars, no horse-drawn carriages, and very few bicycles. A daily bus service to Al Ramlah was the main getaway. However, the railway gave the town's residents a cheaper and a more convenient mode of transportation, especially to Yafa, Haifa, Jerusalem, and beyond.

A short winding road connected the train station to the center of town. After a steep ascent, the road negotiated two bends—the first at the peak of a hill, where a row of tall poplar trees bordered it on each side, and the second around the villas, where it finally straightened out into a course that took it across the train tracks, less than a mile north of the train station, in the direction of Al Ramlah. That was the road David took on his way home.

During his walk, David replayed, in his mind, the scene he had witnessed a few minutes earlier at his father's office.

Although he was aware of the conflict between the Palestinian Arabs and Jews, he vaguely understood the historical origin of that conflict and certainly not the political complexities of world affairs at that early time of the year 1948. He couldn't comprehend how, all of a sudden in his estimate, hell broke loose when until then Arabs and Jews and Muslims and Christians lived happily and harmoniously together. He never considered his Jewish and Muslim friends to be aliens in that land. On the other hand, he thought the British were the only true aliens. Being of Egyptian descent, he naturally sympathized with the Arabs, and was confident that they would prevail and that life would return to its normal, peaceful flow. That conclusion didn't comfort him as much as he desired. He saw religion as the source of that conflict. Although he never doubted the presence of God, he had some unanswered questions about the necessity of having three religions, each claiming the same God as its own but continuously fighting with the other two. He believed that Christianity was the correct and the true religion, yet he couldn't help but question the providential justice that, according to his understanding of the New Testament, had doomed his Jewish and Muslim friends to eternal hell. Unable to resolve the mysteries around him, his thoughts turned to school and education, especially that he was about to graduate from his four-year primary school in a few months.

By then he had reached the front door of his house, one of the larger villas in town. His mother was playing the piano. When he opened the front door, he immediately recognized one of Chopin's polonaises. David's mother had already introduced him to classical music and played for him other popular piano pieces. She had also taken him to a live performance at the opera house during one of their visits to Cairo, Egypt. At that time, she told him about an Italian musician who wrote an opera for the opening ceremony of that magnificent theater. David was so impressed by that live performance, as well as by the history of the Cairo Opera House, that he decided to become a musician when he grew up. His mother appeared to be happy with his decision and promised to buy him a violin if he passed his final exam with distinction.

David was next to his mother before she became aware of his presence.

"David, what are you doing here?" she asked, with a sudden start. "You're supposed to be in the train on your way to Kantara."

He managed to recount to her the scene that had unfolded earlier in his father's office. At the end he said, "Father told me to go home until he found out when the train would be allowed to leave."

"Oh, well," said his mother. "I am happy to see you anyway. Come to the kitchen, and I'll fix you something to eat. It has been a long time since you ate your breakfast. You must be hungry by now."

David's mother grew up in the city of Luxor in Upper (Southern) Egypt. Similar to most of the girls in well-to-do Christian families, she had attended an all-girls missionary school run by Catholic nuns. Most of the teaching was conducted in French. Arabic and English were also taught but as secondary languages. Music, in addition to housekeeping and embroidery, formed a major part of the girls' education, and that's how David's mother acquired her knowledge of classical music and learned to play the piano.

All that education wasn't meant to prepare the girls for higher education, let alone a career; not too many girls went to the university or worked outside the house at that time anyway. David's mother didn't even have a chance to consider a career or to go to a university; she was married to a cousin of hers at the young age of sixteen, as was the prevailing custom in rural Egypt. However, she nurtured her dreams and aspirations to instill them in her children. Out of her four children, one boy, Joseph, was attending the University in Cairo; one girl, Victoria, was married and living in Kantara, Egypt; and another girl, Julia, who was fifteen, was still living in the house and attending a nun's school at Al Ramlah. David, the only one who was born in Al Lodd, had been boarding with his sister Victoria in Kantara since he was sent four years earlier to attend the primary school there. His father had insisted on an Egyptian education. "You should ultimately go to Cairo University, just like your brother," his father said when David had mastered all the knowledge available to him at the Al Lodd school.

"I don't know why they held the train at the station." David's mother seemed to be thinking aloud as she preceded him into the kitchen. She deliberately turned around, looked at David, and added in a clearer voice, "Your father will let's know the whole story when he comes home. This reminds me that I have to prepare the food. I wasn't planning for you to eat lunch with us, but I have enough for you too. Go ahead and clean the vegetables until I prepare the meat. Your father likes a balanced diet with meat, rice, vegetables, and fresh salad. I should be able to finish everything before he comes for his lunch and siesta."

David's father didn't come home, not for his lunch or his siesta, that day. Too many things were happening at the train station.

···

After dispatching David to the house, the stationmaster turned to the British officer for the promised explanation.

"Now, can you tell me what's going on?" he asked.

"Our secret service has learned that the Jewish Irgun organization is planning to raid this train on its way to Egypt," the British officer said.

"But this doesn't make sense," the stationmaster said. "Most of the passengers on this train are of British origin. The Irgun must have known that. They must have also known that the British are the ones who promised this land to the Jews and made it possible for the United Nations to adopt the partition resolution."

"It is more complicated than that," the officer said. "You know that the Jews air-raided a train before and dynamited many rails across the country. I'll explain all that later, but for now, let's do what the commanders want us to do."

The British officer led the way out of the office, heading to where his car was parked. The stationmaster followed in his footsteps.

"Fine, what do they want?" the stationmaster asked.

"They want us to fit an antiaircraft gun on this train."

"How do they want us to do that?"

"They left it up to me, and that's where I need your help."

"We can place the gun on an open-platform car."

"I thought of that too, but an open-platform car would be inconveniently exposed and uncomfortable for the crew. Instead, modifying one of the enclosed-cargo cars to accommodate the crew and to enable them to use the gun whenever the need arises would be a better option. What do you think?"

"I see your point. We can remove part of the car's roof and put the gun on a platform under the created opening. Then the crew can use the rest of the car as living quarters, and they can maneuver the gun through the hole in the roof."

They were at the side of the car by then. The British officer opened its door, sat in the driver's seat, and looked at his companion before he started the engine.

"Excellent idea," he said. "How long would it take to modify a car like that?"

"Our workshop has all the necessary tools," the stationmaster said. "Let me work on that right away. In the meantime you can bring the gun, and I'll make sure that it will be fitted properly in the car."

"I'll bring you lunch with me," said the British officer as he was driving away, "so don't leave the station until I come back. We'll eat together, and then I'll explain everything as I have promised." As an afterthought, he added in a louder voice as the car picked up speed, "Tell your wife to keep your lunch for dinner, and if she doesn't mind, I might even join you then. Some music might help us all. So long Bishara."

"So long Jim."

With that much agreed upon, each one went his separate way to execute his part of the project.

In less than an hour, both of them were back in the station. They sat at the desk, opposite each other, to eat their lunch.

"What do you think?" the officer asked after he had swallowed his first mouthful. "Will your car be ready today?"

"I don't know for sure, but I doubt it," the stationmaster said. As he felt it necessary to explain, he added, "Most of the repair shop's workers have already gone home for lunch and their siestas. I have sent someone to bring them back and left detailed instructions on what we need them to do."

"I had trouble at my end too," the British officer said, to the relief of the stationmaster. "Things are messed up now. Our forces have to pull out of Palestine before May 15, when the UN mandate expires. This camp's commander wasn't briefed about the possible air raid on the train, but he is in the process of getting his orders from the high command. Once this is done, we have to take our freight car to the camp instead of bringing the gun here. You well know that I hold an administrative job, not a fighting one. The camp commander trusts only himself to oversee fitting the car with the needed platform and gun."

They sat silently until they finished their meal. The stationmaster finally said, "I have been thinking." Hesitantly, he proceeded to explain. "I am not an expert on warfare, but I thought it might be more advantageous to send the train at night, under the cover of darkness, when it would be a more difficult target for their airplanes."

"I have already discussed that with our commanders. That's why I am not worried about our mutual delay."

Without his siesta and with a full stomach, Bishara could hardly open his eyes. He shook his head to rid himself of the drowsy feeling, stood up and walked to the window. British soldiers were moving aimlessly in and out of the stationary train and along the platform in apparent boredom, as a lazy atmosphere overhung around the station.

"Now that we have nothing else to do but wait," Bishara said as he returned and sat down across from the officer, "can you explain to me what's happening? I still don't understand why the Jews are attacking the British when you are their benefactors?"

"You apparently refer to the Balfour Declaration."

"Yes, I do. You promised the Jews a state of their own in somebody else's land, and then you influenced the United Nations to accept the partition of the country. I don't think that makes…"

The British officer interrupted him. "It is true," he said, "that the British promised a national home for the Jews in Palestine when they issued the Balfour Declaration in 1917. But if you are familiar with this declaration, it didn't say a 'Jewish State' but a national home and even that was conditioned on the requirement that '…it does not prejudice the civil and religious rights of non-Jewish communities.' You might think that that was not the right thing to do, but don't forget that the world was facing a great war in 1917. And to win that war, we had to get all the help we needed, including that of the powerful Jewish establishments of the world. The idea of a Jewish state was not a British idea. It only came about when the Arabs and Jews refused to live peacefully together in one state. The introduction of the partition solution was necessary to separate them into two different states, one Jewish and one Arabic."

"Still," the stationmaster said, "the UN mandate allowed the British to manage Palestine and 'to establish the necessary infrastructure to enable it to ultimately become an independent state.' It was an Arabic country then, and you should have left it as Arabic as you had received it."

"Don't blame it on us, my friend. Your Palestinian neighbors are the ones who sold their land to the Jews. Of course there were other factors involved in creating this Palestinian problem. The world affairs are much too complicated for you and me to resolve. But let me go back to your original question."

At that moment, the assistant stationmaster entered the office, interrupting the flow of their conversation. He reported that the workers were back in the shop and they had already begun to work on the car as planned.

"That's fine," the officer said. "Let's know when the work is finished, so I can deliver the car to the military camp. We do have enough time to finish the whole bloody thing before sunset and send the train on its way by night time."

The stationmaster summoned the office boy and ordered him to prepare two cups of tea. "Don't put sugar in the tea," he told the boy. This precaution was necessary because he knew that his British friend did not put a lot of sugar in his tea as the Arabs did. He was anxious to return to their conversation.

"Back to my original question," Bishara presently said. "Why do the Jews attack you when you have already helped them that much?"

"OK," the officer said. "Let me explain a few things to show you that we, the British, are not as bad as you might think."

The office boy returned with two cups of tea and tried to serve them, but the officer dismissed him. He put one spoonful of sugar in his own cup, and with a smirk on his face, he put three spoonfuls in his companion's cup. "I don't know how you drink tea with that much sugar. It masks the true taste of the tea. You might as well drink honey instead," he said, sarcastically.

The stationmaster didn't answer. He was familiar with this often-repeated observation. He was more anxious to go back to their conversation rather than to get distracted by senseless talk about tea and sugar. The officer didn't wait for a response, and as if he knew the meaning of his companion's silence, he took a few sips of tea and resumed his explanation.

"You wonder why the Jews attack us," he said. "Of course you are referring to their attacks on the King David Hotel in Jerusalem, the blowing up of bridges, and the dynamiting of the rail system. All that anti-British terrorism is due to the fact that we are trying to be fair to all parties. You blame us for the Balfour Declaration, but you close your eyes on our sincere efforts to limit the Jewish immigration. When you were selling your land to the Jews, we were patrolling the shores to limit the number of Jewish immigrants. This is the evenhanded-ness of the British that you do not see or acknowledge. It is this evenhanded-ness that brought us under the terrorist attacks of the Jews. Did I answer your question?"

"You did," the stationmaster said. "But when you say that we don't under-stand you, the fact remains that you are the superpower, and you pretend to be the benevolent ruler who does what's good for his subjects. You created the problem from the beginning. First you persecuted the Jews in Europe, then Germany killed most of them, and now you want to get rid of the rest and ban-ish them in someone else's land."

"Wait a minute," the officer said in anger. "Did we really create the prob-lem? To tell you the truth, it is you—both Jews and Arabs—who are set on your own fixed religious and nationalistic ideas. You are really fossilized rem-nants of an old and rotten world. For all I care, let both of you fight your own fight. Soon, we'll be pulling out of here, and the field will be open for all of you Arabs to join the civilized world and eliminate the rest of the Jews. Good luck."

By then the night was advancing, and, without a moon, a darkened sky hung over the station. The few light posts that lined the platform gave a faint, yellowish glow to the air. Very few British soldiers were milling around, as the majority were slumbering inside their cars. In the stationmaster's office, a tele-phone rang. The officer picked up the receiver and brought it to his ear. He immediately straightened up and motioned to his companion.

"Let's go," he said as he led the way to the repair shop.

The modified car was ready. A locomotive was brought to pull it to the military camp, bring it back fully equipped with the gun, and attach it to the train. In the meantime, David was summoned from the house, and everything was ready for the train to depart to Egypt under the cover of darkness, as planned.

"I love it," David said to himself when his father led him to the end of the train and delivered him to the conductor in the caboose. "It would be exciting to travel in the caboose," he mumbled, more to himself than to anyone in particular.

"You shouldn't travel by yourself with things going on as they are," his father told him. "I'll feel better if you stay with Uncle Mohammad just in case something happens to this train."

He then turned to the conductor and said: "Mohammad, give your signal for the train to leave. Go in peace, and God be with you."

The conductor turned a knob on top of his lantern, and its red light changed to green. He waved it out of the window, and soon enough the train slowly pulled out of the station. The locomotive picked up speed, as the smoke from its furnace and the steam from its boiler drifted backward on top of the trailing cars, as if to cover them with a warm blanket on that cold and dark January night. The gun-car was attached immediately behind the locomotive followed by five passenger cars, filled to capacity with British soldiers, and a few cargo cars for their equipments and arms. The caboose formed the end of the line.

After the train had left, the stationmaster and the British officer sat opposite each other, satisfied with the day's work. The train station became empty and desolate. An eerie hush floated over the place and its occupants, as if all the day's commotion and noise were packed in an extra car and shipped away with the departing train.

"How about a drink?" the stationmaster asked the officer. "I am sure that my wife has prepared a good dinner. Do come with me for a drink and a healthy Egyptian meal."

"I don't mind that at all, although I feel that I have imposed myself on your household quite often."

"Nonsense," the stationmaster said. "You know that you're welcomed in our home any time."

The stationmaster finished his paperwork, closed the office, and led the way out of the station to where the officer's car was parked. Once settled in his seat, he turned to the officer.

"You accuse us of being fossilized remnants of an old world," he said. "You have to admit that we have fossilized with us a few commendable traditions. And the famous Arab hospitality is one of our cherished traditions. So don't feel guilty. Come and enjoy."

...

David sat on a metal bench that was bolted to one side of the caboose. The conductor sat on a chair next to a metal platform on the other side. A single mattress and a few blankets were laid on the cold, metal floor, and an oil lamp, suspended from the middle of the ceiling, was scattering more shadows than light. A ghostly silence hung over the place except for the double click-click sound of the train wheels as they rolled over the gaps between the jointed rails. Click-click—click-click, *the monotonous, familiar, and predictable rhythm that might have been a beat for,* David thought, *a galloping melody.*

The conductor raised his head from a stack of papers that were piled on his metal desk. "Here we are, David," he announced. "Are you afraid?"

"No," David answered. "Actually, I am more excited than afraid. This is the first time I get to travel in a caboose, and I don't think that there will be any raid on the train as it is traveling in the dark."

"I agree with you," the conductor said, as he handed a package to David. "Your father brought this canteen for you. You can eat now or wait for a few minutes until I finish my paperwork. Then we can eat together."

"I'll wait," David said. "I am not that hungry."

When the paperwork was finished, they opened their canteens on the table after it was appropriately cleared. The conductor insisted that David used the only chair in the car, while he sat on the bench with his open canteen on his lap. Neither person said anything until they had finished their meal.

"Do you remember me, David?" the conductor asked, breaking the silence.

"Of course I remember you. You are Uncle Mohammad from Al Kantara," David answered him. "Your daughter goes to school with me and…"

"That's right," the conductor broke in.

"And my father talks a lot about you and your wife," David continued, as if he had not been interrupted.

"We worked together in Al Kantara," the conductor said, "before your father was transferred to Al Lodd and before you were born. Actually, my daughter was born nine months after your father had left. She was born in Al Kantara, and you were born in Al Lodd in the same year."

"I know," David said.

With nothing more to say, the conductor told David to sleep on the mattress, as he himself would be busy with his work, especially when the train made its stops at the coming stations. He gave David one of the blankets and spread another one on his shoulders.

"Have a good night, David," he said, as he sat on the chair and returned to his paperwork.

"Good night, Uncle Mohammad."

David stretched on the mattress and covered himself with the blanket, but his thoughts kept him awake. He remembered the many trips he took back and forth on this route during the previous four years. He challenged himself to guess where was the train at any given moment by the change of its speed, the screeching of the wheels when they negotiated different curves on the tracks, and by what he could see through the window of the caboose, even on a dark night like that one. He figured out that the train would soon reach Rakhaboat, the last Jewish settlement in that stretch of Palestine. He knew that he wouldn't fall asleep until they had passed that settlement. If an air raid happened, he reasoned, it would occur before the train reached Egypt. But it wasn't fear that kept him awake; it was the worry that if a raid happened while he was asleep, he would miss a whole new experience.

He recalled a previous experience when he was traveling in a first-class compartment with the beautiful daughter of a neighboring Egyptian family. She was on her way to a high school in Cairo, and he was on his way to Al Kantara. He felt then that he was in love with that girl, despite the difference in their ages. She talked to him in the sweetest voice he had ever heard, tenderly touched his hand, and even embraced him and let him sleep on her chest. He only regretted that he fell asleep on her chest and didn't stay awake long enough to enjoy the warmth and softness of her body. *Did she love him, at least during that trip?* He wondered. He didn't know for sure but he hoped that she did.

He raised his head to look through the window. He could see a few stars dotting the night sky but nothing else except silhouettes of trees and faint light from distant buildings—nothing like the empty desert of Sinai, the desert that had always intrigued and fascinated him.

He remembered another trip when the train was crossing the Sinai Desert on a clear summer day, and he was alone in the first class compartment. The sand dunes receded one after another, and each one looked different yet made from the same heap of yellow sand, decorated by undulating lines as if intentionally painted by the creative hand of the desert's wind. He lost his book-bag to the desert during that trip. When he extended his hand out of the compartment's window and felt the strength of the wind, he decided to test that force by exposing his bag to it. He emptied the book-bag, grasped it by its handle and thrust it outside the window. The wind was too strong for his hand that he lost his grip on the handle. He saw his book-bag fly backwards and ultimately vanish in the vastness of the desert.

"We passed Rakhaboat," the conductor said when he realized that David wasn't asleep. "Soon we'll reach Gaza."

David was too tired to resist sleep any longer. In his dreams, he saw himself sitting in the Coptic Cathedral in Yafa, smelling the intoxicating incense and listening to the melancholic chants of the monks who lived in a nearby convent. Suddenly his dream took him to Jerusalem where he found himself sitting in the square across from the Church of the Holy Sepulcher, as Abyssinian monks came out with their torches to announce the resurrection of Christ. He was pushing and shoving the crowds around him when the rhythmic click-click sounds and the rocking movements of the train stopped. He woke up to find himself in Gaza.

Refreshed by the Mediterranean breeze and excited by the dim lights of the city, he followed Uncle Mohammad out of the caboose for a walk on the solid, stationary platform. British soldiers were going in and out of the train, and he practiced his English with some of them. Every now and then, he noticed soldiers and women in uniform, hugging and kissing without any apparent shame or embarrassment. Nobody around him seemed to mind that open display of affection and sensuality. David wondered if moral norms varied in different countries and with different people. It must be an accepted behavior for the British to kiss in public, while it was completely immoral to do so in his conservative society. He bought a pretzel just to dismiss those thoughts from his mind.

His walk took him to the other end of the platform where the locomotive was spewing steam and smoke. He lingered there, oblivious to the passage of time, as if a mysterious force was attracting him to that locomotive. A bell rang, announcing the imminent departure of the train, and brought him back to reality. He reluctantly retraced his steps to the caboose.

When the rhythmic click-click sounds and the rocking movements resumed, he couldn't fall asleep again. He was anxious to be awake when the train arrived at Rafah, the first stop in Egypt.

Rafah was a small village at the border between Egypt and Palestine. Its train station was a primitive one, without even a platform. Thus, when the train stopped there, David jumped out of the caboose onto the soft desert sand. His excitement, walking on Egyptian soil, made him heedless to the chilling effect of the desert's early morning breeze. He even convinced himself that the Egyptian air felt and smelled refreshingly different than that of Palestine. The surrounding palm trees looked like ghostly-shadows in the dawn's dim light but to his eyes, they compared favorably to the olive groves of Palestine. On the other hand, he had to admit that nothing in Egypt rivaled the buyyaras (orchards) he used to visit with his family in Haifa, where he picked and ate fruit directly from the trees. The Bible, he concluded, was correct when it described Palestine as the land of milk and honey.

The next stop was Al-Areesh, an oasis by the Mediterranean. When the train stopped there to fill its tank with water and replenish its coal supply, David took a walk between the palm trees that were rising near the seashore. He wondered how the sandy soil and the salty water could have sustained those majestic trees. Having no answer to his question, he walked aimlessly until he found himself next to the locomotive. *What factory could have built such a huge machine, and how much steel must have been used to build it?* He questioned himself, but he had no answer to these questions, either. The engineer, recognizing him as the son of the Al Lodd stationmaster, invited him to climb the ladder and satisfy his curiosity. Through an open door to the furnace, he saw an intense fire bellowing from the burning coal, spewing black smoke and soot. Soon, his eyes started to burn, and a spasm of coughing forced him to return down the ladder and run away from the locomotive. As he stood nearby catching his breath, he saw some workers busily hauling more coal for the furnace and others filling the locomotive's water reservoir through a long, wide fabric tube that looked like a huge elephant's trunk. Even as he had seen that ritual many times before, his fascination never diminished. "*I am in love with this machine,*" he whispered as he walked back to the caboose.

After Al-Areesh, the train left the Mediterranean coast and continued its journey deeper in Sinai until it reached Al Kantara, where a new and transformative chapter in his life awaited the young boy.

KANTARA

Al Kantara Shark was a sprawling town on the eastern (shark) side of the Suez Canal, opposite its twin city, Al Kantara Garb, which was on its western side. The shortened name, Kantara, was conventionally implied as referring to Al Kantara Shark, the larger of the twin cities.

As in the case of Al Lodd, Kantara was another settlement for the service of the railway network that the British had established all over the Middle East. It was the main border crossing between the Nile valley and the Sinai Peninsula, as the Suez Canal formed a man-made barrier between the two, extending from the city of Suez, at the tip of the Gulf of Suez in the south, to the city of Port Said on the southern shore of the Mediterranean Sea. The difference between the two parts of the country was nowhere as dramatic as in the area of the two Kantaras, where a canal from the Nile River, after traversing the eastern desert, reached the neighborhood of the Suez Canal and ran parallel to it in a northerly direction. The river fertilized and nourished the soil around Al Kantara Garb, making it possible to reclaim that stretch of desert for agriculture. The result was something like a painting with different hues of green: lush expanses of verdant crops and vertical, ragged lines of variable inclines topped with the distinctive, umbrella-like fronds of palm trees in contrast to the barren, yellow sand that extended eastward as far as the eye could see.

Kantara was divided into three separate residential sections, conveniently positioned around the heart of town, the "old" cargo train station and its servicing facilities. An upper-middle class residential section, called Al Ghotoose, was located in the immediate northeastern side of the station. Similar to Al Lodd's design, most of the buildings in Al Ghotoose consisted of two attached family homes with much the same stonewalls, red-tile roofs, and fenced gardens. The usual large, separate villas of the British and the upper-class managers of the railway were lined up at the edge of that section.

Farther north, separated from Al Ghotoose by a sizable stretch of desert, was the largest residential section of town, Al Ezba, or the Farm. Those two sections shared a mosque and a communal oven in the intervening desert but nothing else. In contrast to Al Ghotoose, the residents of Al Ezba were blue-collar workers. Its houses were mostly single-family homes of thick, mud-brick walls, and its streets were narrow and unpaved. It wasn't unusual to find heaps of a mixture of rotting mud and straw fermenting in the larger intersections. When that mix became ready, or cooked, it was poured into rectangular wooden molds and left to dry and bake in the sun until it would be used for new buildings or home renovations. Al Ezba had no running water. Instead, there were communal wells with manual pumps sparsely scattered at strategic locations. The well-to-do residents of Al Ezba hired a waterman, who would, during each trip to their homes, carry two buckets of water, one on each end of a curved, wooden bar that he balanced on both shoulders. But the ones who couldn't afford to hire a waterman carried the water themselves. Each home stored that water in a Zeir, a huge pottery urn, which cooled the water and gave it its renowned sweet and fresh taste. There were no sewers either; a sewage disposal man came every day with his donkey-drawn cart, collected the sewage in a big tank from the toilet pit of each home, and disposed of it in a cavernous septic field far out in the desert. There was also no electricity; kerosene lamps supplied the light, and kerosene stoves or wooden fires supplied the heat for cooking.

South of the old train station was a large expanse of desert supporting a cinema at one side and a Coptic Complex, consisting of a church, a garden-café, and a primary school at the other.

The Souk (market), or the commercial section, was the most southern part of town. Mostly tradesmen and merchants lived there. In the Souk, free spirit and lack of planning reigned. The streets were winding, and the houses were irregularly built from any available material. Cafés, groceries, bakeries, and another cinema attracted the townspeople for shopping, socializing, and entertainment. A mosque, a Roman church, a nonsectarian primary school, and the only high school in town were its well-known landmarks.

Another train station, the New Station, was located south of the Souk, immediately on the eastern side of the Suez Canal. A customhouse was attached to this train station, and a quarantine complex rose across the street from it. The only paved road in town, which connected the two strain stations, sneaked its course through the intervening desert.

The word *Kantara* in Arabic means "*a bridge*," which was an apt name for the two Kantaras, as most of the traffic between Sinai and the valley passed through them. However, a real bridge, the Ferdan Bridge, spanned the Suez Canal a couple of miles to the south and carried the trains to the main land of Egypt.

A large British military camp, encircled by a barbed-wire fence, sprawled at the edge of town. A paved road and a separate rail track connected it to the outside world.

Religion dominated the lives of the town's inhabitants. It also dictated how and where they were buried. Accordingly, two separate cemeteries were necessary, one for the Muslims and another for the Christians. There was also room for two more cemeteries for foreigners, made necessary during the Second World War to bury the British and the Allies' soldiers, mostly from India and Kenya, who died in battle in that part of the world. The one for the British was close to Al Ghotoose, where running water was available. It was more like a fenced park with sandy walkways, straight lines of crosses, and rows of tall, majestic eucalyptus trees. The Indian cemetery, on the other hand, was buried somewhere far off from town in the hot, arid desert north of El Ezba, without any landmarks or definition. Very few of the townspeople were aware of its existence.

Two large ferries transported people, animals, cars, and goods between the east and west, without charge. Privately owned Feluccas, or rowboats, were also available for a fee to those who were in a hurry to cross the canal, especially when the ferries had to wait and give the right of way to the ships' traffic.

It was to the new passenger station that the train delivered David to Kantara. After disembarking from the train, he hurried through the customhouse and stepped into one of the horse-drawn carriages that lined up outside the station.

"To Al Ghotoose," he instructed the driver as he settled down in his seat.

When the carriage negotiated the curve around the Souk, David reminded himself of the distance he would have to walk when he would join the high school in that section of town. He figured out that that distance must be double what he had been walking daily for the previous four years from his home in Al Ghotoose to his primary school at the Coptic Complex. The thought of a longer daily walk bothered him, but as the spire of the Coptic Church started to appear in his visual field, his reflections shifted to his present. Next day would be the start of the second semester of his fourth and final year at the Coptic Primary School. He wasn't sure if he would welcome that end or might come to regret it. He intuitively believed that the remaining few months would determine the outcome in his favor.

By then the carriage was crossing the rail tracks at the last bend in the road as it approached Al Ghotoose. Soon enough, he was at the front door of his house. His brother-in-law, Sami, came out to receive him and carry his suitcase. His grandmother and his sister Victoria, with her child in her arms, were waiting for him inside the house. David's homecoming didn't require any elaborate ceremony, as everyone was used to his coming and going between Kantara and Al Lodd. Without any formalities to mark a division of time, the midterm vacation imperceptibly flowed into the regular rhythm of life, and David acknowledged and accepted that flow.

Sami, who was a teacher at the Coptic Primary School, was already out of the house when David woke up next morning. Like all other students, David started his usual walk to school. Soon his schoolmate Hassan, who lived in El Ezba, joined him. When the two friends reached the cinema, they started sifting through the sand in front of the ticket window–some of the school children had a ritual of stopping there on their way to school and search in the sand for coins that might have been dropped by drunken British soldiers the night before. On that particular day, David was lucky to find a few Piasters (the Egyptian Piaster was equivalent to one cent at that time), which he believed it to be a good omen for a happy and successful day.

Despite its name, the Coptic school had room for Christians and Muslims alike. It was also unique in accommodating girls and boys at the same time, a necessity dictated not by liberal sentiments but by economical prudence, as the small number of female students didn't justify an additional school. However, the separation of the sexes was strictly enforced. Outside the classrooms and during the physical education exercises, girls and boys were separated from each other, and in the classrooms, girls were assigned to the left row of desks, separated from the boys' desks by a *safe* distance. Some of the students had already grown beyond their puberty years, making that separation more necessary.

After the daily lineup for the raising of the flag, the students stayed in line, with their hands extended in front of them for the routine inspection of the cleanliness of their fingernails and the tidiness of their hair and dress. When that ritual was completed, David ran to his classroom and sat at his assigned desk, ready for the first class in the second—and final—semester.

History was the subject of his first class. The history teacher was known for his patriotism and enthusiasm. Although the history of modern Egypt, after the Napoleonic Expedition, was the subject of his assignment, this teacher couldn't help but touch on the current Palestinian problem to project his personal aversion to all European exploitation of Egypt and the rest of the Arab world. Although David was anxious to listen to his favorite teacher, his mind uncontrollably drifted to something else—more personal and pressingly present. The rest of the morning classes passed slowly until the bell rang to announce the lunch break. The moment he was waiting for had finally arrived.

He stood in the schoolyard until the students gathered around him, as was their custom after each of his previous trips to Palestine. This time, he had more exciting stories to tell about his vacation in Al Lodd, especially the scene he had witnessed at his father's office and his adventurous train ride in the caboose. He didn't leave out any detail, particularly the addition of the gun to the train, the air raid that didn't happen, and his excitement for riding in the caboose with "Uncle" Mohammad. He elaborated on the last point with a calculated intention to impress Eva, Uncle Mohammad's daughter, who was standing among his listeners. Despite the strict school rules, Eva was the only girl who dared to join the boys in that gathering—but not for long. Soon she ran away to join the rest of the girls, and David didn't come close to her for the rest of that school day. *There must be a way,* he thought, *that he could approach her and tell her how much he cared for her.* If he was to get her attention, he had to figure out a way to do that soon, as the school year was about to end in a few more months, and he didn't know for sure if he would have a chance to see her after that.

By the end of that school day, he was still too occupied by his own thoughts to join the other boys in their after-school football game. He preferred to have his solitude to find a way out of his quandary. So he avoided taking the paved road for his walk home and took instead the sandy trail, which was isolated, much less traveled, and beyond the reach of inquisitive eyes. As he walked on the soft sand, Eva's face was still vivid in his mind.

Eva was the product of a mixed marriage—her father, Uncle Mohammad, was a Muslim of Turkish origin, and her mother was Jewish. That's why she didn't look like a typical Egyptian girl. Her skin was of a lighter color with a tinge of pink that added a rosy appearance to her countenance. A straight, upturned nose projected from her face and separated two prominent cheeks and two brilliantly expressive blue eyes. Full, reddish lips outlined her mouth, and a square chin added a special strength and character to her face. She kept her blonde hair long and braided it in a single bundle that extended down to her lower back. To the eyes of the schoolboys, she looked like a fairy, untouchable and unreachable, but not to David who was attracted to her and who had a feeling that she was attracted to him as well.

Walking on the desert trail, David was thinking of how he could approach and get the attention of that beautiful girl, when he suddenly heard her voice. She was approaching him from behind.

"David," Eva said, when she had caught up with him. "I saw you walking this sandy trail alone, and I thought it safe for us to walk together."

She remained silent for a few more steps to catch her breath. He remained speechless as if he were paralyzed by her unexpected appearance, despite all his previous planning and preparation for that particular moment—the moment he contrived to be alone with her. Mercifully, Eva saved him from his stupefaction.

"I was listening to your stories at school, and I heard you say something against the Jews," she said, after she had regained her normal breathing. "You know that I am half Jewish. You're lucky to be an Egyptian and a Christian, but I don't know who I am."

She stopped for a moment to rehearse what she wanted to say next. When she had organized her thoughts, she voiced them in one uninterrupted stretch.

"I don't feel I am completely Jewish," she said at last, "because I have a Muslim father. Neither do I feel completely Muslim because I have a Jewish mother. I am supposed to be Egyptian, but I don't look like a typical Egyptian girl. Sometimes I wish I had curly hair and brown eyes like the rest of the girls, but I can't change how I look. It is not easy to be different."

"I am sorry," David said. "I didn't mean to attack all the Jews and certainly not you. I have never thought of you as Jewish, and I always thought of you as being 100 percent Egyptian. Don't forget that with a Muslim father you are more Egyptian than I am, since I am a Christian. You know that we Christian Copts, though we are the pure descendants of the Pharaohs, are looked upon as less Egyptian than the Muslims, who are mostly Arabic." He liked what he had just said, but to throw in a personal touch, he added, "So, both of us are in the same boat."

They slowed down their pace in a subconscious intent to extend the conversation, as the end of the trail was approaching.

"You make me feel better," she said.

They walked silently for a few more steps.

"My father talked a lot about your trip with him," she subsequently said. "He thinks you are a good boy. He told us that himself."

David felt his heart pounding in his chest and wondered if that was due to the exertion of walking on the sand or from the way she said the last few sentences, as if her father's opinion was also her own. There was only one way to find out.

"Eva," he said. "I have been thinking of you a lot. I wish I could see you somewhere where we could talk and be with each other."

She didn't seem to be upset by this direct approach. To his gratification, she said, "You know the British cemetery? I often go there by myself, and I know of a hiding place where nobody would be able to see us. Meet me there after an hour."

They were nearing the end of the sandy trail. David lingered behind to leave a safe distance between Eva and him. Once she reached the paved road, she ran away in a hurry without waiting for his answer.

He was in the cemetery before long, but she wasn't there. When she didn't show up after a few minutes, which seemed to him like an eternity, he started to despair. What if she wouldn't come at all? What if her parents prevented her from going out? Worse still, what if she didn't actually like him but was only playing on his sentiments? Despite all those uncertainties, he kept on waiting.

It was getting dark when he glimpsed her approaching figure. He wanted to run and meet her halfway, but his legs failed him. He wanted to shout and call her name, but he feared that someone might overhear him. Luckily, she saved him from his perplexity by pointing to her hiding place. There they stood opposite each other in obvious perplexity. Finally, she was the one who dared to break the awkward silence.

"David," she said, as she touched his hand. "I am sorry to be late. My father was going out to the café, and I had to wait for him to leave before I could come."

"It's OK," David said. "I would have waited all day and night for you."

"I know," she said, as a confidant smile glimmered on her face. "I can't help but notice how you look at me and always show off when I am around. I care about you too. Actually, I like you." Realizing that she had revealed too much, she stopped. To hide her embarrassment, and after some hesitation, she added, "But this is not why I wanted to see you today. I do have some problems that are bothering me."

David didn't know what to say when she stopped talking. He felt elated by her confession, though somewhat worried by her last sentence. Whatever was bothering her, it should never be allowed to interfere with their newly found intimacy. Still, he didn't know what to say.

"Don't worry," she said, as if she had read his mind. "My problems have nothing to do with you."

Relieved, he regained his courage. "I am not worried for myself," he said. "I only want to be your friend, and if I can do anything for you, let me know. And I'll do it."

They sat next to each other on the soft sand with their backs supported on a large tree trunk that gave them more privacy.

"My family is in a difficult situation after the present conflict in Palestine," she said. "When you told me this afternoon that we are in the same boat, I felt I can talk to you about my family's problems. Some of the townspeople are taunting my mother by calling her 'the Jewess' behind her back. I heard some students call me the same. We are Egyptians, and we have nothing to do with the Palestinian problem."

Suddenly, he realized that religious undercurrents could surface in difficult times like these; being a Christian was sometimes held against him too.

"Of course," he said, but he didn't know what to say next. It took him a few seconds to formulate his thoughts. Finally, he said, "Your father is an Egyptian Muslim. This makes you more Egyptian than I. I am a minority in my own country, and even the students at school don't let me forget that. I know how you feel."

"You don't understand," she said. "It is more complicated than that. You know that my parents are very protective of me. Even before this Palestinian problem, they didn't allow me to socialize with other kids. Now it is worse; they wouldn't allow me to go out of the house by myself, except to go to school. I had to invent an excuse to get permission from my mother to leave the house today."

"This is understandable," he said. "This is a conservative country, and people are especially more conservative when it comes to girls."

"I know," she said. "But it is even worse in my family. There is something wrong with my parents, which I sense but don't know what it is. There is also something that separates us from our neighbors and sets us apart from them. My father prevents my mother from going out or socializing when he's not with her. I guess that's what they call jealousy, but I feel that there is something more than that. One time, I overheard my father accusing my mother of being unfaithful to him. I have a feeling that their marriage might not last for long, which makes me scared and lonely. Would you be my friend and let me talk to you?"

"Oh, how I want to be your friend," he said.

"Then can we meet again tomorrow after school," she said while she was moving closer to him. Without waiting for an answer, she kissed him on his cheek, stood up, and turned to go away. He stood up and reflexively held her hand in an attempt to prevent her from leaving. A strange lightheadedness overtook him, and he felt something moving between his thighs. Compelled by a strong urge, he pulled her to his chest in a tight, forceful embrace. Suddenly with a convulsive jerk, he felt a sticky fluid running down his underwear, and just as suddenly, he released her from his embrace, as if all the energy had drained out of him.

"Until tomorrow, David," she said, as she ran away in a hurry.

"Until tomorrow, Eva," he whispered, more to himself than to her.

Gradually, he realized what had happened. "It did happen. That's what the older boys were talking about," he told himself. Then he whispered again, "Until tomorrow, Eva. You have made me a man today."

That transformation gave David a new confidence and elevated his sentiments to a higher orbit above that of the older boys. Next day, he listened with detachment and indifference when his friends talked about their fantasies and imagined sexual exploits. He didn't participate in their pranks when they congregated in the classroom before the end of the lunch break and the older boys started to write sexually laden sentences on the blackboard. They were so busy with their game that they didn't hear the bell announcing the end of the lunch break. It was only when the teacher was at the threshold of the classroom door that one of the students quickly erased the offending words on the blackboard. A faint image of the writing, though, was still discernible when the teacher started his lecture. Suddenly, suppressed laughter and whispers spread from the girls' corner that forced the teacher to inquire about the cause of the commotion. One audacious girl pointed to the blackboard and started reading the still obvious sentence, "If a boy kisses a girl, she will get pregnant." The teacher had no choice but to stop the lecture, bring in the headmaster and conduct a lengthy investigation. The handwriting on the blackboard was compared to that in each boy's notebook until the two teachers picked up a suspect, who turned out to be one of the older boys in the classroom. Despite the boy's adamant denial, the evidence was enough in the minds of the teachers to convict him. The custodian was called into the classroom, and the punishment was executed immediately. The custodian sat on a chair and held the suspect prone on his lap, exposing his bare feet. The headmaster forcefully hit the boy's exposed feet with a cane, while the other teacher counted, until they finished the required penalty. The boy was helped back to his desk, and the lecture resumed as if nothing had had happened.

Despite that horrible and frightening scene, David still went to the British cemetery to meet Eva. Now that he had established contact with her, he wasn't about to give up in fear of punishment. He reasoned that they would be more discreet and avoid any possibility of being discovered in their hiding place.

This time around, he didn't have to wait for long. She came and greeted him with a kiss on his cheek, but he was determined to avoid any closer contact with her body. An obscure feeling of guilt made him believe that he had committed a sin the previous day and that his pleasurable sensation had violated her sanctity and injured her innocence.

"Maybe," Eva said, "we shouldn't see each other after what had happened at school. I am afraid that someone might see us, and then we'll be in big trouble."

"Don't say that," David said. "We just have to be more careful."

"I made sure that nobody was following me," Eva said. "You cannot be too sure, no matter how careful you are. But I had to come today as promised, especially because I felt depressed following our conversation last night. I'm sorry, David. I didn't mean to bother you with my problems."

"Me too," he said. "I didn't mean to force myself on you."

"Then, we are even," she said. "Actually, I take that back. I do have to bother you. You're a boy, and you're free to come and go and talk to whomever you want. And I know that you go to church and Sunday school. Your religion lets you talk to the priest in confession. I have none of that; I am a girl. I am not allowed to talk to anyone, and I don't know to what religion I belong."

"Eva," he said, "all religions are the same. They acknowledge one and the same God. They teach us Christianity in church, but like you, I am studying the Koran at school. So far as I know, the three religions tell the same stories, call for the same good, and prohibit the same evil."

"Then why do people fight in the name of religion?" she asked. "Even my parents are always fighting their religious wars, and I am torn apart between the two of them. You are lucky to be comfortable in one religion."

"I know. I am lucky to be a Christian. It is the correct religion."

"You see," she interrupted him. "You are as fanatic as the rest of them. That's my point. Every believer is naturally biased to his own religion, and that's the whole problem. I don't know as much as you do about religion, but I wish that people would keep their beliefs to themselves and live happily with each other. If they did, there would be no war in Palestine or in my house."

As it was getting dark, he didn't see the sarcastic smile that covered her face when she asked, "Do you know why you are a Christian?"

"Because I believe in Christ," he said reflexively, unaware of the trap she was setting up for him.

"Not true," she said. "You are a Christian because you were born to Christian parents. Actually people belong to one religion or another by the accident of birth."

"I see your point," he said, as he regained his reasoning power. "Now I can understand why you're confused; you have inherited two opposing religions. But you and I have a lot to learn. To tell you the truth, I don't understand much in either the Bible or the Koran. They are two difficult books to comprehend, but maybe in the future, both of us will understand them when we are older and more knowledgeable. Only then we might be able to make a choice. For now, the war in Palestine is far away from us, and this year we are going to graduate from primary school. We shouldn't worry about the war or religion. Let's concentrate on our studies instead."

"You're right," she said. "It is getting late, so let's go home and hit the books before somebody sees us together. Good night, David."

"Good night, Eva."

He kept his promise; he let her go without receiving a kiss or forcing an embrace. Alone in the cemetery, her words echoed in his head. "You are Christian because you were born to Christian parents."

If religious affiliation, he thought, *was an accident of birth, as Eva had said, then what about what he had been learning in Sunday school? What about his fervent prayers during the mass? What about the rituals he participated in as an altar boy? Was he a victim of an accident of birth, most assuredly like all the believers who attended church every Sunday and the multitudes who gathered in Jerusalem on Easter Eve? Jesus was no accident; his life story was documented. So was Mohammad's.*

David couldn't answer his own questions, but from that moment, the seeds of doubt were planted in his mind. His love for Eva provided the fertile soil that allowed those doubts to flourish.

Maybe in the future, he finally concluded, *they would find a way to marry, despite the religious divide that appeared to prevent that eventuality.* He was certain of that.

...

David went to the cemetery every day, but Eva didn't show up. He recalled all their conversations but couldn't find anything he had said or done that might have offended her. One day at school, Eva managed to slip a note into his hand. He knew then that she didn't return to the cemetery due to a fault of his, but that her parents had prevented her from going out. In their tight-knit community, nothing stays secret; her parents heard about the school incident. Reassured, he was content to be close to her in the classroom and exchange with her secret notes every now and then. With the certainty of his love, he vowed not to expose her to any danger, even if that meant not meeting her in the cemetery or any other place, alone. He was content to be close to her when their families visited to share a meal or play cards.

In the meantime, he found it conveniently distracting to join the other boys in their after-school activities. David especially enjoyed football. The boys had an inflatable leather ball at school, with which they played in physical education class. After school, however, with no leather ball available to them, they constructed one of their own. They stuffed socks with rags, and then they rounded the whole thing with threads until they got a somewhat firm ball. Barefooted, they played their games on the soft desert sand. All they needed were a few stones to mark a goal at each end of a stretch of land and enough players to make two teams.

When they didn't have enough players, David frequently accompanied his friend Hassan for a walk to the Suez Canal, where they undressed to their underwear and descended the stony embankment for a swim. They made sure to swim across the canal and return before any ships approached—an event that would disturb the calmness of the water and create so much turbulence that swimming would be dangerous. When that happened, they would sit on shore, watch each ships as they passed in front of them and wave at the sailors, who would invariably wave back at them.

Excursions to Western Kantara were special treats and equally enjoyable distractions. During those trips, David accompanied his sister and brother-in-law to take the ferry, cross the canal, and buy fresh produce from the weekly farmers' market. He loved to walk between the rows of stalls and watch buyers and sellers barter and bargain in animated gestures. Goats and sheep were slaughtered, and their carcasses were hung from posts to be offered for sale, in whole or in parts. After they returned home, his family would enjoy a freshly prepared meal, and David would be thankful for the generosity of the fertile land of Egypt.

With all those activities, life in Kantara was like a beautiful dream for David, especially as Eva had become the center of that dream. If the Palestinian

Crisis ended and his family stayed at Al Lodd, he was sure to continue his education at Kantara High School in the Souk and remain close to Eva. The possibility of a war and the resulting displacement of his family didn't cross his mind. The consequences of the 1948 Arab-Israeli War weren't in anybody else's mind either. David had to wait for the future to find out his new fate.

THE LAST TRAIN

K antara's new passenger train station was built much later than the old one; hence its name and its modern architectural look. Two platforms formed the body of the station around which a few ancillary buildings were attached. A short arm connected the two platforms on the canal side, making it a dead-end station. A high tin roof covered the whole complex. An office building and a customhouse opened on the northern platform. The customhouse was a vast, high-ceiling space, like a warehouse, enclosing a rectangular, raised counter behind which officers stood to inspect the passengers and their luggage. There was no access to the train station except through that customhouse, an arrangement that made it necessary for anyone going in or out to pass through that space. The only paved road in town, which connected the old and the new train stations, expanded into a wide parking area, just beyond the customhouse, to accommodate the ferry traffic. In front of the station, a stretch of this road was reserved for the horse-drawn carriages, which were the only mode of available transportation. A vast courtyard, enclosed by very high, mud-brick walls, bordered the other side of the road and housed the facilities of the Quarantine.

"*I hope they come on this train,*" David told himself when he entered the stationmaster's office one afternoon in early April. He had been going to the train station every day during the previous week, but still his family didn't come. That day, he walked from school as usual, but with a new and hopeful expectation. "*If I keep on waiting, they are bound to come,*" he reasoned. The stationmaster greeted him as he entered the office. "Hi David, I have good news for you today. I received a telegraph that your family is coming on this train. However, the train was delayed at Rakhaboat because someone had mined the tracks just before the Egyptian border. They have already removed the mines and repaired the tracks. The train is now at Al-Areesh. I expect it to arrive here in three or four hours."

That's the news David was looking for. His patience and perseverance were finally rewarded.

"That's fine, uncle," David said with apparent relief. "I have nothing else to do. I just have to wait."

David left the office to take his usual walk around the station. His romantic fascination with the train stations and the good news he heard from the stationmaster had revived his spirits. Some of the railway employees were obviously busy with their work, but the majority were aimlessly sitting around or just pretending to do something or another. He knew that most of the work that actually needed to be done happened between the arrival and departure of the trains. A sense of satisfaction filled him with peace as he headed to the other end of the platform. He was immediately greeted by the same characteristic smell he encountered in each train station he had ever been to, the same smell that always intrigued him and gave him a strange sense of foreboding and belonging at the same time. As he took his customary stroll, the ever-present peddlers chased him with their insistent temptations.

"Sesame pretzels, eggs, and cheese," yelled the first one, as he followed him for a distance. David had to convince the man that he wasn't going to buy anything, but somehow another one, selling oranges and tangerines, appeared from nowhere. "Sweet as honey are my oranges," the peddler sang in a melodious voice. "Three for one Piaster—what a bargain!" He was so persistent that David had to buy three oranges from him.

The third one was the shoeshine boy with his small box, which he rhythmically tapped with a brush in his hand. "You shined my shoes yesterday," David said as the boy approached him. Thankfully, this was enough to get rid of him. When he reached the end of the platform, he saw the worker, who was responsible for shifting the jointed rails where they converged and diverged as they came in and went out of the dead-end station, sitting in his isolated cubicle. David was content to see that everything was quiet there.

He retraced his steps to the other end of the platform. The peddlers knew, as if instinctively, that he wasn't a potential customer and didn't bother him anymore. However, he couldn't help but listen and enjoy their melodic screams and their rhyming songs.

Once beyond the customhouse, he gained access to the road. "You need a ride to town?" one of the carriage drivers yelled. A simple "no" was enough this time. The high walls of the Quarantine faced him as he looked across the road. Growling noises from quarantined camels reached him as he stood there. He knew that the Quarantine was used to house travelers in case of epidemics before they were allowed to cross the border, as had happened during the last cholera epidemic. He assumed that camels were held there for a similar reason; they must have some transmittable diseases of their own.

Actually, camels were kept there for a completely different rationale, unknown to him. A lucrative trade of hashish flourished across the Suez Canal where it was smuggled from the Sinai Peninsula to the mainland of Egypt. The border guards, who used their own informants and were acquainted with most of the smugglers, intercepted some of that hashish, if it was carried personally or in trucks and cars crossing the canal. However, smuggling it in the guts of camels required a different tactic. These animals were made to swallow sealed pouches of the drug, and then they were slaughtered when they had successfully crossed the canal. Once on the other side of the border, the drug was retrieved from their stomachs, and their meat was sold for food. To combat that practice, the animals were kept in the Quarantine for two weeks. By that time, they would either have died from the drug, if the pouches they had swallowed ruptured in their guts, or they would have passed them through with their excrement. It wasn't a foolproof system, but for the most part, it worked.

Back in the station, David wandered aimlessly until he found himself outside the station again. The scent of crisp, salty air attracted him to the direction of the canal. The hour was getting late in the day and the sun was starting its descent over the western horizon. A few clouds began to acquire a reddish color and to form a mysterious background for the towering palm trees and the minarets that rose up in the air at Al Kantara Garb. Engrossed and absorbed in this scene and the majesty of nature, he didn't notice Eva and her mother sitting on a bench inside one of the ferries. He was thus startled when someone called his name. It was Eva's voice that brought him back to Earth, and what a blessed voice it sounded to him.

"David!" Eva had reflexively shouted his name. Biting her lip in a gesture of regret, she looked at her mother, as if to ask for her forgiveness for that daring move. Without thinking, David managed to get into the ferry just before its gate was about to close, as if an invisible magnet was pulling him in. The ferry was a large, floating platform with its center reserved for trucks, cars, and animals. A long metal bench was bolted to the railing that bordered the periphery of a walkway on each side of the central cargo area. A diesel engine was housed at one end, and a cabin for the pilot was enclosed at the other end. A loose chain, reaching to the bottom of the channel, was securely anchored at each side of the canal and threaded through metal wheels on the side of the ferry, thus taking it through a wide arc, rather than a straight line, as it crossed the canal.

"Hi David," Eva's mother said when he had reached their place. "Come and sit down next to me. It will be a while before the train comes. We thought we would pass the time by riding the ferry back and forth. It is a lovely evening. The scenery is beautiful, and the air is fresh. I guess you're here waiting for your family's arrival."

"Yes." That was all he could say.

"We are here waiting for my husband," she said. "I happened to learn from the stationmaster that this train might be the last one to come from Palestine.

I hope that my husband is on it. He should be because he was scheduled to work on this train, even before he had left for Palestine."

David wanted to impress them with the added information he had. "I heard that someone put explosives under the tracks at the Egyptian border," he said. "They held the train at Rakhaboat until they had removed the mines and repaired the tracks. The train must have passed Al-Areesh by now."

Noises from a nearby felucca, heading in the opposite direction, interrupted their conversation. Its passengers were singing a patriotic song that celebrated the bounty of Egypt and reflected the militaristic sentiment of that time. A derogatory cadenza, aimed at the Jews, trailed as the felucca sped away. The words could be heard by anyone who was listening. "You, the Jew, you, the Jew, put your head in the stew." Those words reminded David of Eva's lamentations the first time he met her at the cemetery. With a wrenched heart, he thought it wise to say something to divert their attention away from the offending song.

"We must be at the mid point of the canal," he said as the distance between them and the felucca was growing and the derogatory song was fading away.

"The other ferry is across from us, heading in the other direction," Eva said excitedly. "I always wondered how these ferries stay their course and how the currents don't carry them away from their destination."

"I know why," David explained. "Each ferry is attached to a metal chain that keeps it in its course and moors it to the shore."

"You are a smart boy, David," Eva's mother said.

The last stretch of the crossing passed without any further conversation as they became engaged in watching the final approach to the western shore. At last, the ferry gave a succession of loud thuds as it gradually settled in its confining place. Everyone on board disembarked, except them.

"We should be waiting in the station when the train arrives," Eva's mother said, as she motioned for them to stay in place for the return trip.

It was already dark when the ferry started its easterly journey. Nothing was said for a few minutes until David felt a compulsion to impress them again, as the "good boy" Eva's mother had said he was.

"It's too dark now to show you how the chain I told you about is attached to the shoreline," he said. "But still we can walk to the place where that chain is attached and appreciate the massive structure and the huge metal ring that holds the chain. I sometimes wonder why the whole thing doesn't fall apart under the push and pull of the ferry."

"It is OK, David. We believe you," Eva's mother said. When she realized the hidden intention of his remark, she added, "You are a very observant boy. My husband thinks highly of you. He told us about your last trip with him. He said that you were courageous and well behaved. Your parents must be proud of you."

He felt as if he was floating in a blissful air when he heard those words, especially that his beloved Eva heard them too. With uncharacteristic shyness, he found it difficult to respond, and his restrictive, conservative culture kept him silent. But the mother had something more in her mind.

"We don't have any more time to waste. I like to be in the station when the train arrives." She then directed her concerns to something else. "It is April now," she said, "and next month will be the end of your school year. Both of you should be concentrating on your studies to be able to pass the final exam."

"I am," David said. "I know that Eva is also. There is somewhat of a competition between the two of us in the classroom, and I am sure that both of us will do well."

"I hope so," Eva's mother said.

The usual thud of the arrival of the ferry shook them from their seats. They stood up, steadied themselves, and walked out of the ferry and onto the solid ground.

"Good night, Aunt and Eva," David said in a faint voice, as if he were in a daze. "I hope that Uncle Mohammad comes on this train."

When the train finally arrived, David was standing on the platform, look-ing through the windows of each passing car in search of his family. Suddenly, he jumped with joy when he saw his mother's head extending out of a window. He ran to that window and walked alongside of it until the train came to its final stop. His mother grasped his head in her hands and kissed him on both cheeks. When he was free from her grip, he looked inside the cabin and saw the smiling face of his sister Julia, but his father wasn't there.

"Where is Father?" he asked.

"He didn't come with us," his mother answered. "I'll tell you everything on our way to your sister's house, but now help us with our luggage. Let's go out of this train; it has been a long, tiring trip."

He ran to the end of the car where he entered through the door and walked the length of the crowded corridor until he reached the compartment where his mother and sister were waiting for him.

"Where are your sister and her husband?" his mother asked, when she realized that they were not waiting for her.

"They didn't come to the station today," he answered. "They came with me every day during the last week but not today. Their little baby is sick, and they had to take him to the doctor. They will be waiting for you at home."

A porter was summoned to carry the luggage, and the three of them followed him out of the train, through the customhouse, and onto the street where they settled in one of the waiting carriages on their way to his sister's house in Al Ghotoose.

Nothing is as exhilarating as a carriage ride through the desert in the early spring. That particular night was clear. The vaulted sky was studded with sparkling stars, and the moon, at its fullest, spread its unobstructed light throughout the vastness of the desert. But no one paid any attention to that. David was thinking of his father when he turned to his mother as soon as the carriage started to move. "Why didn't Father come with you?" He asked. "I heard that this train might be the last one out of Palestine. How else would he get out?"

"The British commander wanted him to stay until the last of the British troops pulled out of Palestine," she said. "In a month, the British will be out, and the war will start. Don't worry. Your father knows his way around. He will manage to get out safely."

To their right, the Souk was coming into view. The silhouettes of the mosque's minaret and the spire of the Roman church appeared like two mysterious, giant ghosts, inspiring awe and wonder. Beyond the Souk, and to their left, the Coptic Complex with its church and school loomed at a short distance. David's mother turned to him, as if the place reminded her of something.

"By the way," she said. "How are you doing in school? The final exam is next month. Isn't it?"

"Don't worry, Mom," David answered her. "I have already finished reading all my books, and I am ready to take the exam even now. I plan to review everything again and again during the remaining weeks, so I can get the best grades."

"That's my boy," she said with deeply felt pride.

They passed the school and were approaching the old train station when his mother asked, "What's wrong with the baby?"

"He has a bad case of diarrhea and is crying all the time," David answered. Then he added, "Victoria and Sami felt very bad that they couldn't come to the station to wait for you."

"They did the right thing," she said. "It is not always easy to be parents, but caring for a sick child is more important than any other dispensable social obligation."

When they reached the house, Victoria and Sami were waiting for them at the door. The passengers of the carriage descended quickly, and everybody fell into the outstretched arms of everybody else. The women entered the house, while the men unloaded the luggage and took it inside. More hugging and kissing ensued, as David's grandmother, a widow who lived with Sami and Victoria, joined in the ritual. Nobody minded the loud cries of the baby, who was passed from one pair of arms to another. Everyone was talking at the same time, so it was difficult to understand what was going on until they settled down, as if exhausted from a strenuous ordeal. A more sensible discourse, mostly centered on the health of the baby, prevailed soon thereafter.

A small wood fire in a tin can was blazing in the courtyard. David's grandmother asked everybody to follow her to where the fire was burning. She stood there, enshrouded in a flowing black dress, befitting an Egyptian widow, holding the baby in one arm and a paper effigy in the other. The figures of the attendants in the bright moonlight and the undulating shadows from the flaming fire appeared like ancient ghosts from an old and mysterious fairy tale.

"I was waiting for all of you to be together to go through this ritual," David's grandmother finally said. "We have to exorcise the evil spirits that are making this baby sick."

Nobody seemed to object to what she said or did. She handed the baby to his mother and immediately started to recite verses from the Bible. When she had finished, she punctured the paper effigy several times with a needle and threw it in the fire. She then turned to Victoria and asked her to step across the fire, back and forth seven times. She continued reciting obscure words with each count, until the seven required steps were duly executed. When the ritual had finished, she took the baby back and lead the way to the inside of the house.

David's grandmother grew up and spent most of her life in Upper Egypt where this ritual was practiced generation after generation since the time of the pharaohs. Christianity and Islam failed to abolish these ancient traditions and they inevitably incorporated most of them in their own that nobody could tell anymore what came from paganism and what was brought by modern religions. In any event, David's grandmother was the matriarch of the family, and nobody dared to question the wisdom of her beliefs. They let her have her ritual, and when she was done with it, they resumed their animated talk until it was time for sleep.

As he lay in bed, David reflected on the events of that memorable day. The exorcism he had witnessed was still vivid in his memory. Ghosts and spirits frighteningly materialized in his mind and prevented him from falling asleep. Every time he closed his eyes, he pictured demons floating in the air around him. He had to keep his eyes open in the darkened room to make sure that they were not there to possess his body and torture his soul. All the sermons he had heard told of a devil, evil spirits, and a hell of inconceivable torment. If there were a devil, he reasoned, how would God allow him to spread havoc in the world, incite violence and war, inflict an illness on his nephew, and above all, use religious differences and a set of conflicting cultural beliefs to separate him from his beloved Eva? It was only after he recalled that day's ferry ride and after Eva's image had dominated his thoughts that he reached a more tranquil state. He finally fell asleep. To his good fortune, Eva's presence dominated his dreams, a far cry from the ghosts and evil spirits he was afraid of. He woke up before dawn. Everybody else was still asleep and the house was very quiet. In that calm solitude, Eva remained in his consciousness and his daydreams.

Strangely enough, the baby started to improve the following day, and David's grandmother didn't let anyone forget the part she played in his recovery. The rest of the family was happy to give her the credit.

PORT SAID

The school arranged a day trip to Port Said for the senior class, boys and girls included, as a farewell treat. Early in the morning of the assigned Friday, the weekend holiday in the Muslim calendar, all students lined up in two lines—one for the boys and the other for the girls—at the gate to the ferry in the Kantara Shark terminal. One teacher led each line to a separate section of the ferry. David and Eva glanced at each other with a secretive look that acknowledged the remembrance of a previously shared ferry ride. Each one felt the proximity of the other, and both of them were content to know that they were silently sharing another memorable experience.

The passage of a convoy of tankers delayed the crossing of the ferry; the ships always had the right of way. The students disembarked and lined up on shore, where they stood watching the ships as they sailed in front of them. In its passage through the canal, each ship seemed to siphon the water from the depth of the canal and pile it ahead of it. A deep trough would thus form behind it, as if to expose the bottom of the canal, but soon enough the waters would return to fill this trough and its surface would be restored to its original level before another ship would reach the same spot and repeat the same sequence.

David watched the ships like everybody else, but his thoughts were busy with other things. *What if their different religions became an obstacle, as they surely would, and he wouldn't be able to marry Eva in the future?* He thought. *Wouldn't it be nice to escape in one of those ships to a far away and tolerant country where nobody cared about whom you worshiped or whom you loved? The English people he came across didn't seem to be bothered by religion. They didn't even care about morality as the Arabs did. They kissed and hugged in public places without any apparent shame or guilt. Yes,* he concluded, *an escape to their country would surely solve his problem.* Before he could figure out how to accomplish that escape, the ferry blew its whistle to announce its imminent departure, and everybody rushed on board.

Crossing the Suez Canal was always an enjoyable experience, but on that particular day, it was doubly so for David and Eva. When they exchanged another fleeting glance, they meant to reassure each other that their bond had gained more strength over the previous few weeks, especially after their public and memorable ferry ride with Eva's mother.

The train station at Kantara Gharb was a charming little place with only one platform overlooking the green fields, and a brick office building facing the Suez Canal. The nearby village of the same name supplied the whole area, including Kantara Shark, with fresh produce. David looked at the distant palm trees as they extended straight up to the sky and remembered how he had climbed one of them just a week earlier with his friend Hassan to harvest some of its newly sprouted, supple branches for Palm Sunday service. He thought how strange it was that in a land where religion had carved a deep gulf between its two major groups, that gulf disappeared on a few special occasions—at least in the area of the two Kantaras.

Palm Sunday was one of those special occasions. Christians and a few Muslims headed west to harvest fresh palm fronds and spent the preceding Saturday weaving them into intricate and decorative designs from crosses, baskets, and various fanciful figures. Although the sharing stopped on Sunday morning, it wasn't unusual for a select group of Muslim officials to go to church with their Christian neighbors. To them, Palm Sunday ceremony was more festive than religious.

The month of Ramadan was the other special occasion. Although Christians didn't fast, they did refrain from eating publicly in deference to their neighboring Muslims who fasted the whole day. In a sense, this respectful restraint gave them justification to join in the evening and nightly festivities, if not in the plentiful meal that followed the breaking of the fast after sunset. Following that meal, colorfully clad children walked the streets with multicolored lanterns in their hands, chanting special folk songs to celebrate Ramadan. Through the evening and most of the night, people would congregate in each other's house, in the cafés, or in the streets to socialize, eat some more, or just kill the time with gossip and petty talk. They would hardly go to sleep when the "*Mossaher*" would wake them, as he stopped at each house and called its residents by name, tapping on his drum and reciting famous songs for the wake-up call. The Mossaher would urge everyone to get his or her Suhoor, or the last meal of the night before sunrise and the start of another day of fasting. Most of the Christians and the Muslims who didn't fast participated in the nightly festivities and responded to the Mossaher's call.

Religions aside, one tradition was observed and strictly enforced—the separation of the sexes. This was exactly what happened when the students were in the ferry and on the train. Once they reached Port Said, however, the two teachers led their respective contingents to the same destination, as the history teacher, who happened to be one of those teachers, was supposed to be in charge of the whole historic expedition. He accordingly led everybody to a large square on the waterfront, where the students separated into the two obligatory groups but still within a hearing distance from the lecturer.

Mediterranean cypress and eucalyptus trees stood at the periphery of the square, and cobblestone walkways, bordered by neatly trimmed bushes, converged onto its center. There a statue of de Lesseps, the architect of the Suez Canal, stood high on a tall pedestal, facing the harbor and pointing with his hand to the entrance of the canal. The distinct European features of the statue's face and its posture and gesture reflected the image of a proud figure and, at the same time, a defiant attitude as if to say, "I am the master who conceived and built this canal."

As the Suez Canal had played a major role in the modern Egyptian history, no place was more appropriate to explain that role than under the shadow of the de Lesseps statue.

"If you understand the history of the Suez Canal," the history teacher started his lecture once the students had settled down around him, "and how it was conceived and built, you will understand the history of modern Egypt. We have to begin with the French occupation in the eighteenth century. Anybody knows the date when the French came to Egypt?" When nobody answered him, he turned to David.

"David," the teacher said, "you must know the answer."

"I remember that it happened in 1798," David volunteered, "but I am not sure of the day and month."

"You're right about the year," the teacher said. "It was June 28, 1798, when the French fleet docked at Alexandria."

"Was de Lesseps with Napoleon when he invaded Egypt?" one of the students asked.

"No," said the teacher. "But de Lesseps was in Egypt later on during the reign of Mohammad Ali, the founder of the modern Egyptian Dynasty and whom we had studied previously. However, he couldn't sell his plan to build the canal to Mohammad Ali."

Another student said, "I am all mixed up now. Then Napoleon had nothing to do with the Suez Canal."

"Yes and no," the teacher resumed his explanation. "Napoleon did have the idea of building the canal, but his engineers made a mistake in their calculations. They erroneously concluded that the water of the Red Sea was a few meters higher than the Mediterranean and thus connecting the two seas would have flooded the whole Delta. That's why Napoleon gave up on the idea of building a canal."

"How come," David asked, "nobody, not even the pharaohs, attempted to connect the two seas before?"

"Actually," the teacher said, "the idea occurred to every ruler of Egypt since around 2000 BC, but none of them acted upon it because of the same error of calculation that was in circulation until the time of Napoleon. It was only during the rule of Mohammad Ali that engineers discovered those errors. Ferdinand de Lesseps became aware of this fact when he approached Mohammad Ali to allow him to dig the canal, but Mohammad Ali rejected his request, fearing that the proposed canal might encourage the European powers to invade Egypt. A few years later, de Lesseps saw a better chance to build the canal when Said, his friend and the son of Mohammad Ali, assumed the rule of Egypt in 1854. De Lesseps managed to get Said to sign one of the most outrageous and one-sided agreements in history. In this document, Viceroy Said granted de Lesseps the concession to build the canal. He granted him a stretch of land on each side of the canal, promised to supply free labor, and above all, he agreed to take up 44 percent of the shares of the new canal company when de Lesseps failed to secure all the necessary capital from France. In short, Said mortgaged the future of Egypt to a ruthless and merciless European exploiter. On April 25, 1856, the digging started.

"Ferdinand de Lesseps got his canal for free, while Said died before its completion. It was Ismail who was the ruler of Egypt when the canal was completed."

"I thought that the Ottoman Turks were the rulers of Egypt at that time," one of the students interjected.

"Yes, they were," the teacher explained, "but they ruled Egypt indirectly through their Viceroys, from Mohammad Ali on down. This is another story, but let me go back to the canal story for now.

"Ismail inherited from Said an impoverished country that was still under the rule of the Ottoman Empire, as I have already mentioned, and ransacked by foreigners and aristocratic Pashas. However, his own extravagance hastened the descent of Egypt into bankruptcy. Just for the sake of the useless title of Khedive, Ismail paid a large sum of money to the Turkish Sultan to grant him that title. He then bankrupted his treasury by a frenzy of public works to dazzle the crowned heads of Europe at the opening of the Suez Canal in the year 1869. In Cairo, he developed the present midtown area with its famous boulevards and public parks. He built palaces all over the place, including the famous one in Gezira Island and Kasr el Nil Palace, at the eastern side of the Nile, which became military barracks for the British when they ultimately occupied Egypt. He even established a new city, Ismailia, midway along the canal. For the opening ceremony, he built a classical opera house in the center of Cairo, a facsimile of the European ones, which opened on November1, 1869."

Hassan, David's friend, raised his hand. "I think that Ismail wasn't as bad as you have described him," Hassan said, after the teacher had acknowledged him. "We have to give him credit for all those projects and buildings."

Those comments obviously irritated the teacher.

"You'll understand what I mean when I reach the end of Ismail's reign," the teacher said. "In the meantime, we have to look at all those projects as benefiting the aristocracy and foreigners, not the hard working Egyptians. Now that we have finished with this detour, let's go back to our story.

"The festivities that accompanied the opening of the Suez Canal were a spectacle unparalleled in history. Heads of states arrived from all corners of the world and were lavishly entertained by their generous host, the Khedive. On his expense, they enjoyed the luxuries of Cairo and the splendor of the pyramids. They traveled to Upper Egypt to see the temples of the pharaohs at Luxor and Aswan. Ultimately they were escorted to Port Said for the opening ceremony. From there, a convoy of yachts sailed to Ismailia, headed by Al Mahrousa, the Khedive's own luxury yacht. At his new palace in Ismailia, Ismail entertained his guests with one of the most sumptuous banquets in history. Remember the stories from *One Thousand and One Nights* I told you about? These events sound like one of those stories except that this time, there was no happy ending. In fact, if there is someone to blame for the British occupation of Egypt, it is surely this Ismail. He financed his extravagance by loans he borrowed from the Rothschilds who were a European-Jewish family with tremendous wealth and influence. Just remember their name. They have a lot to do with our historical setbacks and even more with the current Palestinian problem."

He stopped again to collect his thoughts. David took advantage of this hiatus to look in the direction of Eva. He saw her face contort with sadness. He recalled the first time she told him about her religious conflicts, and he felt an urge to hold and comfort her. However, he knew well enough to stay in his place. He managed, though, to look in her direction with an understanding expression on his face. He was gratified when her face relaxed as their eyes met. He knew then that Eva had understood his message.

"Back to the Rothschilds," the teacher continued where he had left off. "They didn't only charge Ismail exorbitant interest, but they also paid him a fraction of the loans as compared to the recorded value in their books. Ultimately, Egypt had to sell its shares in the canal to the British just to pay part of its accumulated debts. Said had granted de Lesseps and the French the concession, the land and the free labor through a one-sided deal, and Ismail had given the British the opportunity to own part of the canal and to ultimately occupy Egypt through his ill-guided extravagance and his financial recklessness."

The teacher then looked at the student who had previously voiced his admiration of Ismail.

"Hassan," he said. "You understand now how Ismail had inflicted much more harm on Egypt than could be offset by all his other accomplishments. At any event, this is the statue of de Lesseps I have been telling you about."

By then, the students became impatient and irritable. Their attention drifted from the teacher to the scenery around them. A few ships were anchored in the open sea, waiting for their turn to cross the canal. Local vendors rowed their small boats in the vicinity of the large ships, selling Egyptian souvenirs to the sailors. Seagulls surfed overhead until they spotted a meal then suddenly dived in a swooping motion to capture whatever they could get. Sea breezes rustled the leaves of nearby trees and produced a melody of natural sounds. The fishy, salty smell made the sensual experience more acute and intoxicating, which made the students less inclined to listen to a serious lecture. Sensing the obvious irritability of the students, the teacher decided to turn his attention to a different and more interesting direction.

"On a different note," he said, "another statue, the Statue of Liberty, was initially offered to Egypt to be erected at the entrance of the Suez Canal, but this wasn't meant to be. The Statue of Liberty stands now in the harbor of New York City, while Egypt ended up with the statue of de Lesseps."

David listened attentively. He clearly remembered the Cairo Opera House, but he didn't know much about Verdi or *Aida*, except for the origin of the Egyptian national anthem. Neither did he know anything about the Statue of Liberty, which, as his teacher had mentioned, was standing in New York harbor in America. He returned to his dream of escaping with Eva on one of those ships, and this time around, he thought about going with her to America, the country that won the Statue of Liberty. He wasn't listening to the lecture when he woke from his daydream as an unintentional grunt came out of his mouth and the teacher was getting his attention by calling his name.

Embarrassed, David found it necessary to say something.

"I attended a performance at the opera house you have mentioned. I also know that our national anthem is taken from Verdi's Opera Aida."

The teacher thanked David for that extra information. But he didn't want to be eclipsed by one of his students. He accordingly resumed his tirade against the British, describing them as usurpers of the canal.

"Then Egypt doesn't own the canal?" David asked.

"Practically no," the teacher said in a bitter voice. "Theoretically, Egypt owns the canal, but a British company perpetually runs it for a fee paid to the Egyptian government. The British actually make a lot of money from the canal, but Egypt gets only a fraction of the income."

"But this is unfair," David said.

"You're absolutely right, David," the teacher said. "Yes, it is unfair. Our country is still under British occupation, although we are a sovereign state with our own king. The British reneged on their promise to grant us independence at the end of the Second World War, but we have no power to fight them. It will take a tough struggle to gain our independence. Don't you ever forget, the British will never *grant* us freedom; we have to earn it by fighting our occupier."

By then, the numbing effect of the surrounding nature and an increasing irritability in the students became too disturbing for the teacher to continue. The two teachers conferred to decide on what to do for the rest of the day.

"Let's split now," the history teacher announced, finally. "I'll take the boys to the beach, and the girls will take a more appropriate tour for them."

He led the boys through the streets of the city. People from different ethnic groups crowded the walkways and shops. Greeks, Italians, Maltese, Armenians, and Lebanese added their own special flavor, but the local character of the city was unmistakably Egyptian. Women with full-rounded bodies and over-flowing dresses exuded sensuality as they walked the streets. Men with their Gallabeyas, the traditional flowing garb of Egyptians, kept busy in their trades. Cafés and eateries were scattered at every corner, where people from disparate origins socialized and conversed animatedly with each other. The tour ended in the fish market.

"This is where you can get the best fish in the world," the teacher said, as he entered the place ahead of his students. "Of course, fish and rice are the main food staples in Port Said."

A Port-Saidy woman, with the curves of her body showing through her dress, passed in front of the teacher, and he couldn't help but look lustily at her. Weakened by a compulsive instinct, he glanced around to make sure that nobody else was listening. Then feeling no inhibitions in the absence of girl students, he couldn't resist a man-to-man talk with the boys. Despite his better judgment, he said that this rice-and-fish diet gave the local women their sensual roundness and sex appeal.

Some of the older boys in the group, encouraged by that pronouncement, felt bold enough to gaze at the sexy women around them and voice their own fantasies, which made the teacher realize the impropriety of his daring comment.

"Come on, boys. Let's cool ourselves with a walk on the beach," he said in a firm voice that left no doubt about his authority.

Very quickly, a more formal atmosphere returned to the group. However, once at the beach, the boys felt free to enjoy a swim in the Mediterranean or a stroll on the sand. After they had enough of both, they followed their teacher in the direction of Port Fouad.

Port Fouad, on the eastern side of the harbor, was the manicured twin city of Port Said, where the foreign managers and the elite workers of the Canal Authority lived. A ferry, much larger than the one in Kantara, took the students and their teachers across the channel and transported them to what seemed to be a different world. Majestic trees lined wide and clean streets that led to immaculate villas with the characteristic Mediterranean whitewashed walls and red-tiled roofs. The cleanliness was unmistakable, and a silent hush gave the space an eerie atmosphere, as if nobody lived there. The whole town looked like a fantasy place that had landed there from outer space. The contrast between the opulent enclave of the British in Port Fouad and the crowded city of Port Said was so obvious that the teacher didn't lose any time to amplify on that difference and to advance his own revolutionary agenda. He continued the history lesson.

"Colonialism denies you not only your freedom but also your country's wealth," he said as the walking tour continued. "Look at how the foreigners live and enjoy the bounty of our country. They harvest the fruits of our labor. They take our cotton crop. They export the choicest of our produce, flowers, and roses. And they keep the best part of our cities to themselves. You can see here how they use the income of our canal to live in luxury, while we suffer from poverty and backwardness."

"Isn't it our fault to let them do that to us?" David asked.

"Of course it is," the teacher said. "The fact is that our rulers are content to join the British in looting our wealth and suppressing our people. Our political parties are corrupt, and our elections are fraudulent. The Wafd party is trying to implement some reforms, but it is run by wealthy aristocrats and controlled by feudal interests. The working class is the real power in any country, the source of its wealth, and the builders of its future. Unless we educate all our children, feed our own people, and build a true democracy, nothing will happen. A socialist revolution is our only hope for the future. Now we are busy fighting Zionism. It is left up to your generation to get rid of colonialism and establish a free and truly democratic and socialist system."

The lecture ended when they reached the central park of Port Fouad, a large beautifully landscaped public place. This was the destination for the girls as well, but the traditional separation of the sexes continued to be strictly enforced. Accordingly, the girls quietly sat down in a distant corner, while the boys scattered all over the park. Some of them played racket ball, others football, and a few stayed close to the teacher to continue the political discussions.

At the end of the outing, the students took their seats in the ferry on their way back to Port Said. They were approaching a ship when David realized that, unlike the situation in Kantara, Port Fouad's ferry wasn't attached to a chain. It was free to maneuver its way in the busy traffic of Port Said's harbor, as its big size, heavy weight, and a much more powerful engine enabled it to keep a steady course in the turbulent currents that were created by the passing ships. *How could he accomplish his planned escape?* David thought, as he saw some of the boat peddlers going up and down those ships.

"Can someone like me get a job on one of these ships?" he asked his teacher as they were sitting in the ferry.

"This depends on your trade and experience," the teacher said. "If you are a sailor or a cook and you have the right connections, I guess you could find a job. I know of a doctor who worked on one of the passenger ships. He visited many countries and then settled in America, after he had married an American woman."

David wasn't thinking of marrying an American woman. To live in America with Eva was all that he wanted.

"But can you stay in America if you are not married to an American woman?" he asked.

"I guess you can if they give you a visa," the teacher said. "But who wants to live in America? Not too many Egyptians would willingly leave their country."

"I am just wondering," David said aloud. But his inner voice was saying, *I would.* He looked at Eva and saw her face brightens with a smile. Her eyes glimmered with an unmistakable message: she was listening to the previous exchange, and she understood what he was aiming for. *Dear Eva,* he told himself, *there is still hope for us.*

A joyous surprise was waiting for him at home: his father had returned from Palestine. As excited as he was by the sudden appearance of his father, a more personal and pressing issue claimed his total attention—a mysterious and overwhelming urge to see Eva kept on haunting him. He recalled the conversation he had with his teacher during the ferry ride in Port Said Harbor. Something about the big ships and emigration made him see a possible escape from the religious and cultural impediments in his future relationship with Eva. He could run away with her on one of those ships and end in America like that doctor his teacher was talking about. During the train ride back to Kantara and up until he reached home, he considered every possibility he could think of for that escape. Finally, he concluded that an escape at their age was impossible, but it could be done in the future. How could he discuss all those possibilities with Eva? *I must see Eva.* That mysterious voice kept echoing in his head until he found himself inside the British cemetery, without knowing how he ended there.

He sat under their favorite tree in utter confusion. The world around him was dark and silent. The day's warmth had started to dissipate by the dropping temperature of the desert's early night. Where he was sitting, the sand felt progressively damper and colder, until it induced a chill all over his body. Alone and with nothing around him but tombs, he became frightened by visions of spirits and ghosts. He was about to run away when he heard someone approaching him. Even before seeing her, he knew that she was not another apparition. It was Eva who materialized in front of him in real flesh and blood.

"I knew I'd find you here," she whispered as her face was approaching his and her lips were getting closer to his ear.

"I, too, knew that you'd come," he said and touched her all over, as if to make sure that she wasn't an apparition. "Eva, my father is back from Palestine, but I couldn't stay long with him. Fortunately, everybody was excited by his sudden appearance that I managed to leave the house unnoticed. It's strange; I had a strong urge to see you. "

"Me too," she said. "I know now that there is some mysterious thing that binds us together."

"I know that too. Today, I figured out a way to overcome the force that might separate us. There is hope for the future."

"I know that as well," she agreed. "I happened to overhear your conversation with the teacher on the ferry."

"Then you know that we can escape in one of those ships and immigrate to America. We can get jobs on one of those ships, even scrubbing the floors."

"Not now. Not at our age. Maybe in the future," she said.

"You have reached the same conclusion as I. Now I can see hope for us," he said then firmly grasped her shoulders as if to illustrate what he was about to say, "Eva, I always believed that there is a mysterious force that binds us together."

"Silly you, how could you have doubted that until now? I have believed in this force from the beginning."

"Eva, I love you."

"I love you too, David," she said as she turned around to leave, "Don't try to keep me any longer."

When he kept his grip to prevent her from leaving, she freed herself, determined to leave. "I have to go home, David. Good night."

Her voice faded away as she disappeared in the dark. She wasn't there to hear his response, but still he whispered behind her, "Good night, Eva."

REVERSE EXODUS

The unexpected arrival of David's father called for a special celebration. The following evening, Sami suggested an outing to the club. He invited David to join them, as he was about to leave the house with Bishara.

The club was actually a café, but calling it a club attached some importance and distinction to it. In fact, it was the fenced courtyard between the Coptic Church and school, where the elite men of Kantara socialized around cups of tea or coffee and indulged in unending games of backgammon and dominos. The school headmaster, some of the teachers, and a few of the railway employees were the usual customers. Although it was part of the Coptic Complex, it wasn't exclusive to Christians; a few Muslims were regular patrons there.

An arbor, covered with grapevines, occupied a sizable part of the place and made it possible to sit under its shade in the hot summer days. Bare electric bulbs, suspended from stretched wires, gave an eerily dim light in the dark desert nights. Members of the club sat immediately under these bulbs whenever they wanted to play their games. The non-players usually took their chairs to more isolated and dimmer corners to conduct their never-ending discussions, which usually touched on any imaginable topic that happened to excite their fancy.

On that particular day in April, the weather was mild, and the evening air was fresh and fragrant with the scent of jasmine that covered the club's fence. No less than a dozen men gathered around Mr. Bishara as he sat down under the arbor, accepting their greetings and good wishes. Once the ongoing games of backgammon were finished, the tea and coffee consumed, and the necessary greetings and formalities done, everybody turned to the distinguished guest. They were eager to listen to the story of his escape and to find out what he thought about the coming war, as they saw in him a credible witness and an authority on the subject. David sat next to his father, anxious to hearing more details than the shortened overview he heard the previous day.

"I don't know how I made it. But the adventure is over, and I am here at last," Mr. Bishara started his story.

"Didn't I tell you to come with us in the last train that left Palestine?" Mohammad, Eva's father, questioned him.

"Yes," Bishara said, "but we didn't know at the time that it would be the last train out of Palestine. Besides, I couldn't leave without the explicit permission from my superiors. Once the Jordanian army pulled out of our area—God knows why—I knew that I must run away regardless of what my superiors said. Soon, there will be war allover the land. That's for sure."

"You really think that there will be a war?" someone asked.

"Of course there will be a war," Mr. Bishara said. "I have already seen fighting between the Palestinians and the Jewish settlers, and by the middle of May, the Arab armies will join the fight. Haven't you seen the Egyptian army on its way to the borders with Palestine?"

Everybody agreed on that assessment. After a long and heated discussion, Mr. Mohammad interrupted the conversation by asking the gathering to quiet down. He then said, "Let's hear from Bishara how he managed to get out of Palestine."

"It's a long story," Mr. Bishara started. "As I was saying, once I saw the Jordanian army pulling out, I didn't feel safe anymore. It wasn't a question of getting out but of how to do it. The rail tracks south of Al Lodd were sabotaged, and no trains were going to Egypt. When I declared my intention to leave, a Palestinian and two Egyptian friends joined me in this exodus. First we walked to Al Ramlah, where we took a bus overloaded with Palestinian refugees on their way to Gaza. We were packed in every available space. Amid crying children, screaming women, and smoking men in that confined environment you would have suffocated or gone crazy. However, just a few miles from the Rakhaboat, the bus broke down. Everybody lined up along the road for the inevitable walk to Gaza.

"My friends and I separated from the rest of the refugees and headed to the train tracks with the intention of getting help from the Rakhaboat's stationmaster, who is a Jew and a friend of mine." He stopped to look at Mohammad. "Mohammad, I am sure you remember Cohen," he said.

Without waiting for an answer, he continued his story. "It was getting dark, but I knew the way to Cohen's house. Fortunately, he was home. He received us with open arms and offered us food and a place to sleep. The next morning he directed us to a place where a trolley was kept on a side rail track and invited us to use it for the last leg of our trip. 'Don't worry. The Jewish forces wouldn't bother you as long as you are heading out of Palestine,' he reassured us.

"He was right. Every Jewish patrol we encountered allowed us to proceed after they had found out our identity and destination. Each one of us took a turn working the lever of this trolley, propelling it progressively forward until we ultimately reached Gaza. Our Palestinian friend separated from us to stay with a relative of his in town, and the rest of us stayed with the Gaza's stationmaster."

Another serving of tea interrupted his story. A dry desert breeze wafted through the courtyard and steered them into a contemplative silence, while they sipped their mint-flavored tea.

"This is what I like about this place." Mr. Mohammad was the first to break the silence. "You have to admit that we have the best of everything: good friends, nice town, beautiful weather, and peaceful nature. Something is mysterious about the desert that inspired the Arabian poets to enrich our culture with wonderful and voluminous poetry. As the classical Arabic poet, Emre'ee Al Kice, said…"

"No poetry tonight," one of his friends interrupted him. "As much as we like to hear you recite your poetry, I think that we should listen to the rest of Bishara's story."

The others agreed, as Bishara sipped the last drops of his tea, cleared his throat, and resumed his story.

"Well, Mohammad," Bishara obligingly said. "You know Gaza as well as I do. It does have the charm of the desert you're talking about, but it also has the mysterious wonder of the sea. The sea breeze, with its characteristic smell, blows over the city and mingles with the desert air to give you a combined feeling of romanticism and adventure." He paused for a while, as if to contemplate this line of thought.

David listened to his father's speech and wondered at its eloquence. He dismissed his earlier decision to become a musician and decided to be a poet instead. *Or maybe he would be both,* he thought.

"We stayed at the house of the stationmaster," Bishara finally said. "We showered and had our dinner, then we sat on the porch facing the Mediterranean. After our rough and exhausting trip, it felt like we were in heaven. Nothing is as refreshing as a cold shower, clean clothes, full stomach, and the company of friends. However, our joy was marred by the prospect of war and above all by the plight of the Palestinian refugees who were arriving at Gaza in droves. The next day we went to town to seek our Palestinian companion. He was in tears when we found him. 'Come and see what happened to my people,' he said, as he took us to the outskirts of town where refugees were crowded everywhere. Although some of the refugees were lucky enough to have friends who housed them in their homes and others had some means to rent a place or erect their own tents, the majority was left to fend for themselves in the open air. We saw children with tattered garbs playing in the sand, oblivious to what was happening around them. We saw women collecting scraps of firewood and starting fires to cook their meals. We saw men sitting on the desert floor, helpless and burdened with defeat. In the entire place you could sense a disaster waiting to happen."

"But why did the Palestinians leave their homes?" David asked. Everybody looked at David, as if they were seeing him for the first time. Embarrassed by their surprised attention, he wished he had never spoken, but he was soon relieved by his father's response.

"This is a good question, David. I knew that some Palestinians had sold their land to the Jews, but those were only the wealthy ones. The rest should have stayed and fought for their homes as you have just suggested. I said that to my Palestinian companion and asked him the same question. I learned from him that the Zionist Irgun organization was conducting a terror campaign by burning Palestinian villages and massacring their inhabitants. He told me about a particular village, Der Yassein, where that terror was at its most barbaric brutality. Naturally, other Palestinians feared for their lives and ran away. You see, David, fear is our worst enemy."

A heated discussion prevailed after Bishara's explanation. Some men cursed the Jews, and others denigrated the Palestinians for their passivism. It was Mohammad who finally settled the argument.

"Don't worry," he said. "The Arab governments will join their forces to fight the Jews and return the Palestinian refugees to their homes. You have seen our Egyptian army marching across Sinai and establishing its base at the border with Palestine. The Syrians are poised in the north and the Jordanians in the east. Come May 15, when the British mandate expires, the overwhelming multitude of these armies will victoriously march across Palestine, defeat the Jews, establish an Arabic Palestinian State, and force the United Nations to reverse its partition resolution. Palestine is an Arabic country, and it will stay that way for the Palestinians."

Everybody agreed with that assessment. However, Mr. Bishara kept his silence until someone asked for his opinion. Despite some lingering doubts, he could not ignore the superiority of the combined Arabic armies.

"You are right, Mohammad," he said. "We will be victorious. The refugees will return to their homes, and Palestine will remain a unified Arabic State. And now that we have solved this problem, let's call it a night and head home. See you all in the morning."

David felt that he had grown rapidly during the last few weeks. Eva had inducted him into manhood. The trip to Port Said, the subsequent confessions at the cemetery, and the discussions at the club had delivered him to adulthood. *His future with Eva didn't look that bleak after all,* he concluded, as he went to bed on that night.

THE FINALS

B y the end of April, the school year was winding down. David, like all other school children, was busy studying his books in preparation for the final exam. However, too many things were happening that distracted him from giving full attention to his studies. His home was like a beehive with people coming and going. Also the war in Palestine was imminent, and the Egyptian army crowded his town as it marched to the battlefield.

One day his father took him aside after returning from a short trip to Cairo.

"David," his father said. "I'll lose my job as soon as the British Mandate expires. However, I'll get a pension from the British government. In addition, I found a job as a manager for the trucking branch of our family's transport company. Mother and Julia will accompany me to Cairo where I managed to rent an apartment big enough for all of us. You'll stay here until you finish your exams, after which you'll join us in Cairo."

Going away from Eva wasn't in David's mind, but he knew well enough to conclude that he had no choice but to do whatever his father had already decided. Still, he pleaded his case. "I thought I'd stay in Kantara for my high school," he said. "The school here has an excellent reputation."

"I know," his father said, "but Cairo has much better schools. And at this stage in my life, I want to have all my children under one roof. Victoria has been away from me since her marriage, and I have to accept that. Joseph never lived with us—God knows for how many years. I let you stay in Kantara for the last four years, so you could get a better education. This time around, the better education is in Cairo, where you'll stay with me and with your mother."

David listened to his father with respectful attention. His father's voice was sad, but the expression on his face was stern. David knew that the decision was final, but he reassured himself that the move wouldn't necessarily doom his relationship with Eva. He would surely return to Kantara to visit his sister and keep in touch with Eva. Moving to Cairo wouldn't be the end of Eva, as he had initially thought. He concluded that, at least his father's man-to-man talk with him represented another milestone in his growing-up experience, and he felt ready for a new chapter in his life.

"I am happy that you all are leaving." David finally said. "I don't mean that in a bad way, but it has been very hard for me to concentrate on my studies."

"I understand," his father said.

The distraction didn't end by the departure of his family; the movements of the Egyptian army continued for a couple of more weeks. Convoys of army trucks and tanks traveled the main road on their way to the old train station for transport to the front line. A festive atmosphere enveloped the soldiers and the town's inhabitants alike as if the march was nothing more than a parade to a guaranteed victory. Nobody doubted the superiority of the Egyptian army, especially that it was going to face the "enemies of God," the terrorist bands of the inferior and infidel Jews.

David didn't think of the Jews as inferior. He remembered his Jewish neighbors in Al Lodd to be hard working and industrious people. Neither could they have been the enemies of God, for Jesus himself was a Jew. He became torn apart between his own beliefs and his unquestioning patriotism. However, his sympathies were decidedly patriotic. With the certainty of the ultimate victory, it was natural for him to join other students and chant with them, "God is great," "Victory will be to the Arabs and death to the infidel Jews," even when he knew that as a Christian, he was also considered an infidel.

His daily walks to school brought him closer to the soldiers and their machines. One day, a number of disabled vehicles drew his attention. He approached one of them, which happened to be a tank with a rusty body and a leaky underbelly. A lone soldier stood nearby with a cigarette in one hand and a rifle in the other.

"Good morning, private," David greeted him in an attempt to start a conversation.

"Good morning," the soldier returned the greeting.

"Is there anything wrong with your tank?" David asked.

The soldier scratched the back of his head, looked at the tank, and then turned to face his questioner.

"I don't know," he answered. "It stopped suddenly in the middle of the road. My companion went to get help from the repair crew."

"Can I ask you a question?"

"Go ahead."

"What would happen if the tank stopped in the middle of a battle?"

"It'd be an easy target for the enemy. That's what would happen."

"But if this happened, you could lose the war."

"No way, one tank doesn't determine the outcome of a war. Don't forget that we have a large number of tanks."

David turned his eyes to other tanks that were similarly idling at the side of the road and couldn't help but ask another question. "I see. But if more and more tanks became disabled, you could really lose the war."

"This is completely out of the question," the soldier indignantly said. "Remember, we're fighting a band of terrorists. They have a smaller number of fighters and much less equipment than us. This war is going to be an easy walk."

Reassured by this response, David envisioned this particular soldier trium-phantly walking in the streets of Al Lodd.

"I was born in Palestine," David said. "Think of me when you reach the town of Al Lodd. That's where I grew up. Be careful not to bomb our house, which is one of the villas in the center of town. We want to go back at least to bring our belongings."

"I'll keep that in mind, but I can't know where my unit will end in the land of Palestine. I wish it would end in Jerusalem where I could visit and pray in the Al Aksa mosque."

"Oh, Jerusalem is a beautiful city. You'll love it; I assure you."

The repair crew arrived at the scene, and David had to run to his school. But the image of that soldier and his disabled tank remained vivid in his mind all day. He thought of his Jewish friends and wondered if this particular soldier would kill one of them. Or one of them would kill him. His only experience of war was during the Second World War, but he was too young then. He vaguely remembered the air raids when the entire townspeople would flee and hide in the underground shelter. He remembered his frequent escapades to that shelter when he used to take his Jewish girlfriend, undress in the dark, and play the mating game with her. That excitement wasn't the same as the one he felt when he embraced Eva. The convulsive climax that he felt with Eva was completely different from the uneventful end of his childhood experiences. Nothing of that magnitude happened in the shelter.

When the day of the final exam arrived, the students took their assigned seats in a large tent erected for the occasion in the school's courtyard. He easily found his way in every subject. Finally, he was drawing a colored landscape for his art exam when an air-raid siren sounded.

"Nobody moves," yelled the school's principal. "It could be a false alarm."

Only one lone airplane circled the sky, but no explosions followed. Soon enough they heard the second interrupted siren announcing the end of the raid, and nothing materialized. Eventually, the exam was over, and the students gathered outside the school to compare their answers. David was happy with his performance and made sure to verbalize his satisfaction when Eva was within hearing distance from him. On his way home, he managed to get close to her.

"Can we meet in the cemetery?" he whispered.

Her answer was more satisfying than his performance in the exam. "I'll see you in the cemetery this evening," she said.

That evening, they ran into each other's arms and embraced for a few seconds. Their eyes met. Without saying anything, their heads moved forward and their lips touched. Inexperienced, they didn't know what to do next. A touch was all they could manage, but a touch was more exhilarating to them than an experienced full-blown kiss. When they ultimately parted from each other's embrace, they were left more with a sense of guilt than with one of fulfillment. Everything happened so fast that David, despite his arousal, didn't reach the climax he had experienced before. He didn't wet himself, and for that he was grateful.

Eva was the first to break the silence. "How did you do in the exam?" she asked.

"Very well," he answered. "How about you?"

"Very well in every subject, except Arabic," she said. "I developed a mental block. My father always forces me to learn more about the language and poetry. Maybe I was afraid to disappoint him, but maybe I did well without knowing it. The results will tell."

"I am not worried about you. You definitely know your Arabic, and I am sure that your marks will not disappoint you or your father."

Their previous sense of guilt disappeared as they silently walked to their hiding place holding each other's hand in a tender and affectionate grip.

"When are you going to Cairo?" Eva was the first to break the silence, again.

"How did you know?" he asked.

"There are no secrets in this town," she said.

"I don't know when I am supposed to leave," he said. "I guess I have to wait for the result of the exam and get the certificate in my hand first."

"That's it then," she said, with a sigh. "You'll have a new and exciting life in the big city, while I remain here." After some hesitation, she added. "You're not going to forget me, are you, David?"

"Of course not," he said. "Don't forget that my sister still lives here. I am sure that I will come back to visit her. Five years at the high school will pass quickly. After that, you will be going to the university in Cairo. Then we'll be together again."

"I don't know if my parents would let me go to the university," she said. "But we don't have to wait for five more years to see each other."

"This is not what I meant," he said. "I told you that I would come at least once a year to visit my sister. We'll see each other then."

"I hope so. But for now, would you promise to meet me at least one more time before you leave to Cairo?"

"I promise," he said. "In the meantime, I'll see you at school when they announce the result of the exam and hand us our certificates."

"I'll see you at the graduation then," she said.

She withdrew her hand from his, gave him a quick kiss, this time on his cheek, and ran away.

"See you at the graduation, Eva," he whispered as she left.

At the graduation ceremony, his name was called first; he was at the top of the class. Eva's name was the second to be called and Hassan was the third. As their families gathered after the end of the ceremony, he found himself close to Eva. By a firm handshake to congratulate each other, they reaffirmed their commitment, and when he casually mentioned that he would be leaving to Cairo next day, she understood his message.

That evening they met in the cemetery for the last farewell. They silently held to each other. This time around, when their lips touched and they tasted each other saliva, they instinctively opened their mouths to get more of the same taste. Although they were fully dressed and inexperienced, the warmth of their bodies filled them with powerful pubertal rush of blood that triggered a climax even without actually engaging in a complete sexual act. Eva convulsed with pleasure, and David felt the familiar sticky fluid between his thighs. Relaxed at the end, they sank into a blissful state as if all their energies had drained out. When their heavy breathing subsided to a comfortable pace and their hearts stopped thudding in their chests, they looked at each other in contentment.

"David, this is a wonderful feeling." She couldn't help but speak her mind.

"Oh, yes, I know. Is this your first time?" He asked.

"Yes. I never had such an experience before. Did you?"

"Yes, I did." He hesitated a little, and then said, "It was with you. Remember the first time we met in this cemetery? We embraced just before you left me. It was then that you made me a man. This time it is my turn to make you a woman."

"I am your woman—you just have to marry me," she laughed.

"You are my woman, and I know that someday you'll be my wife," he reassured her. "You remember the ships that were crossing the canal when we went to Port Said?" He asked. "They gave me the idea of an escape. When we finish the university, we'll take one of those ships and go to a distant country where people are free to do what they want."

"You told me this same thing before. It might not turn out to be that simple," she said. "Suppose I don't go to the university. Suppose that my parents force me to marry someone else. Suppose you change your mind…"

"Stop that," he interrupted her. "I promise I'll never change my mind. As far as the rest of your suppositions, your high grades will convince your parents to let you finish your education. Just keep up your grades, and I am sure they will be happy to send you to the university rather than force you to marry. The rest will be easy."

"I'll do my part if you promise to do yours," she said.

They held each other in a final embrace.

"That's it then," she said as she withdrew from his arms. "So long, David."

"So long, Eva."

He stood there as she disappeared from his sight. He tried to run after her. But his energy failed him, and he had to sit down under a eucalyptus tree. He raised his eyes in a silent prayer, but the moonless sky faced him with utter darkness. He couldn't see except a few shiny stars through small openings in the trees' canopy. Neither could he hear anything except the rustling sound of the leaves as they responded to a faint breeze. He closed his eyes as if to communicate with something bigger than him, and he became aware of a transcendental harmony that was reassuring and comforting. Peaceful at last, he went home to sleep his last night in Kantara.

CAIRO

C airo wasn't in David's mind when he boarded the train at Kantara's new train station; the separation from Eva didn't leave him any room to think of the new life he was about to undertake. Everything in his past became valuable because of Eva's presence in it, and nothing in his future would be meaningful, except if she would be part of it. Only momentarily did he think of religion as an obstacle between them, but he never thought of the possibility of losing her—not for their different religions and not for the distance that would separate them. They would work out something to overcome their religious differences, and he was sure to visit Kantara in the coming years, see Eva, and keep their relationship alive. Somehow he felt that their bond was too firm and too permanent to be broken by either of these factors—or even time.

That line of reasoning gradually comforted him. Only then was he able to notice and enjoy the progression of scenery as the train proceeded along its journey to Cairo. Leaving Kantara's station, the train took a wide circle in the desert to perpendicularly approach the Suez Canal. Soon enough, it crossed the Ferdan Bridge, and from there on, it was cruising through the green fields of the Egyptian countryside.

As Kantara receded farther and farther, he couldn't help but think of the coming chapter of his new life in Cairo. He recalled his previous journeys to that city when he went with his parents to visit their relatives and spend their vacations with his older brother, Joseph. He wondered who would be waiting for him at the train station. Suddenly, he became frightened by the possibility of finding himself alone in the vast and crowded city. *Someone will hopefully be waiting for me*, he reassured himself.

It was already dark when the train approached Cairo. David looked out of his compartment's window as he began to feel a mysterious vibrancy, exciting and threatening at the same time. The distant city lights, in a colorful and magical show, appeared to be mystifyingly suspended in the darkening sky, and the city's humming sounds became louder and louder as the train slowly came to its final stop.

His brother was thankfully there to receive him with open arms and to lead him through the crowds, along the length of the platform, and out of the gate, until they were seated in one of Cairo's blue taxicabs.

"To Shoubra," Joseph instructed the driver.

Shoubra was a large district of Cairo. A small bridge, above the rail tracks, connected it to the train station and a short tunnel to the midtown area. Two parallel streets ran its whole length. The main one, Shoubra Street, the wider of the two, was famed as the most chaotic street in Cairo, for it supported two tram tracks in its middle that left only a narrow stretch on each side for the buses, the cars, and the donkey-drawn carts. The other street was called Terr'a (Canal) Street because it was originally the location of a canal from the Nile. Side streets connected these two main streets and branched out to all corners of the densely populated district. Nobody knew why Christians gravitated to Shoubra, but it was a known fact that a sizable number of them lived there. Coptic and Catholic churches in addition to parochial schools were more evident in Shoubra than in any other part of Cairo. A Catholic convent was also one of its famous landmarks.

The taxi crossed the bridge and maneuvered its way through Shoubra Street, miraculously avoiding the trams, buses, cars, donkey-drawn carts, and the multitude of pedestrians. Still, their taxi had a minor fender-bender, which was resolved by shouting and screaming, after which each party went on its own separate way, as if nothing had happened. Finally they reached home, a six-bedroom apartment on the second floor of a two-story building in one of the side streets of Shoubra.

"Here we are, my children," David's mother said after the customary and ritualistic greetings. "At last, all of us will be living together as a family."

"True," Joseph said, "but I wonder how long this will last? It is time for me to get married and be independent. Now that I have a law degree and a good job in the transport company, I am ready to make my own family."

"Of course," his father said. "But you don't have to move out for that. This apartment is large enough for two families. I have already discussed everything with your uncle, and he agrees that it is better for his daughter to live with us after the marriage."

"I don't know if this would be the best arrangement for us," Joseph said.

"Nonsense," the mother interfered. "She is only a child. You don't even want to wait until she finished high school. At sixteen, she wouldn't be able to handle the responsibility of having her own place. Both of you need our financial support and help until you are able to stand on your own feet. That's what families are for."

"I see your point," Joseph said. "In that case, go ahead and arrange for our marriage as soon as possible. She is my cousin, and she wouldn't feel as a stranger in this house."

"Your uncle and I will arrange for everything, as long as we have settled this issue," the father ended the conversation with this pronouncement.

That's what families are for, David recalled his mother's declaration as he went to his room. But he wondered what it would be like in his case. It wouldn't be an arranged marriage like his brother's, but the issue of religion would present an insurmountable obstacle. Somehow, he reassured himself, something would work out in the future. His immediate problem was clearly not marriage but education. His worries soon gave way to the excitement of living in the city and with his family. His father had already told him about Tawfikia High School. He was supposed to go there in the morning and put in his application.

The next day David woke to the sound of a piano. There was no piano in his house; his mother had left hers at Al Lodd. When he became fully awake, he realized that the music was coming from across the street. Looking through the window in his room, he could vaguely see a young woman sitting at an upright piano in the opposite apartment. He figured out that she must be a few years older than he was.

Julia entered the room at that moment, and when she saw who he was looking at, she said, "Oh, this is Magda, my classmate. You will get to meet her one of these days, as our two families visit each other quite often. But now, take your shower while I prepare your breakfast. I'll take you for a tour around our neighborhood and show you your future school."

The music suddenly stopped, as Magda came out to the balcony.

"Julia," she yelled across the narrow street. "Did your brother come from Kantara?"

Julia leaned over the windowsill to answer her friend. "Good morning, Magda," Julia said. "Yes, David is here now."

"That's nice," Magda said. "I am happy for all of you. What are you planning for today?"

The two girls continued their conversation across the street. They finally agreed that Magda would join in the neighborhood tour.

"You'll like Magda," Julia said as she closed the window. "She is a very talented girl. As you can see, she plays the piano, but her main interest is painting. You don't mind if she joins us?"

David didn't answer. Eva was the only person he was thinking of as a companion for a city tour. However, he couldn't help but notice how freely the two girls were talking with each other, not only across the street, but also within a hearing distance from everybody else. *Cairo,* he concluded, *must be a more liberal place than the conservative Kantara he was used to.*

"Don't tell me that you're not interested in girls," Julia said, with an obvious surprise at his silence.

"Not really," David replied, and that was all he could say. His secret would remain a secret for now.

Magda came after he had finished his breakfast, and the three of them went out for the introductory tour. They walked the length of Shoubra Street. First, they passed the girls' school alongside its high, stone fence that concealed everything inside it. He learned that it was called Bon Pasteur, a private school run by Catholic nuns. That was the school his sister and Magda were attending. They continued the tour until they reached an elaborate church complex, which reminded him of his favorite monastery in Yafa. He learned that what he was looking at was the famous Saint Teresa's convent. A high, iron fence enclosed an immaculately landscaped garden where a large statue of the same saint stood at its center and a church bordered it at its inside corner. His sister told him of miracles attributed to Saint Teresa and of how people of every faith converged on that convent looking for further miracles and cures. She described how this place would be ablaze with lights around a centerpiece of the nativity scene during the Christmas season in a production that attracted multitudes of visitors. On their way back, they stood at the corner of a large intersection, where major department stores were housed in large and architecturally ornate buildings. People around them crowded the sidewalks and overflowed into the street, in competition with the already jammed traffic. To David's perception, everything around him seemed to be oversized, overcrowded, and frighteningly threatening. At the end of the tour, the two girls left him in front of his future school, after he had assured them that he would find his way back to the house.

Just one block away from his house, Tawfikia School was a few feet recessed from Shoubra Street. A high and elaborately designed iron fence, not much different than that of Saint Teresa's convent, surrounded the school on all sides. David passed through a wide iron gate and walked a long passageway that was split into two lanes by a central, grassy island. Palm trees towered on each side behind a well-trimmed row of hibiscus bushes. Bougainvillea trees spread their purple flowers as they climbed a fence at the periphery. When he reached the administrative complex, he was directed to the admission office. He submitted all the required documents and finished with his application. He then explored the school grounds. Beside the countless classrooms and a large cafeteria, there were gardens, a soccer field, and a few tennis courts. Everything looked larger than the manageable grounds of his old school in Kantara. After all, he reasoned, Cairo is a much bigger city, and this school is one of its best.

He spent the rest of the day in the house, where his mother and sister were busy preparing the main meal of the day, which was traditionally served in the early afternoon. Without refrigeration or processed food, each meal had to be prepared from ingredients freshly bought every day. Peddlers with their donkey-drawn carts made the shopping easy. People listened to their calls and knew which produce each peddler was selling by the melody of his song and the tone of his voice, even if they didn't actually see what was on his cart. More conveniently, women didn't have to leave their apartments to do their shopping; they stood in their balconies, dropped baskets at the end of long ropes, and hauled up what they had bought after heated and ceremonious transactions.

David was left alone to explore the house. In his brother's room, he was faced with a voluminous library that his brother had already shown him and given him permission to borrow any book he wanted. He browsed through the books, took one that captured his attention, and sat down to read it.

It was the story of the Mayo Brothers, the two Americans who practiced medicine in Minnesota, performed surgeries bordering on the miraculous, and finally established what became one of the most prestigious medical centers in the world—the Mayo Clinic.

That was the beginning of a long-lasting reading habit that contributed more to David's education than what he learned at school. All summer he kept reading more and more books indiscriminately. He read books on religion, literature, history, music, and any other subject that drew his attention. For the most part, he retained only a fraction of what he was reading. Nonetheless, he persisted in his quest for knowledge with the conviction that he was getting something valuable out of each book. A book on Mary Curie, the Polish scientist who discovered radioactive radium, drew his attention, and brought back to his memory the Mayo brothers' story. From then on, he became fascinated with medicine and determined to become a doctor himself. After all, didn't his history teacher say that his friend, who had found a job on one of the ships and settled in America, was a doctor?

Magda's presence became another constant in his life. As a neighbor and a friend of his sister, she was a frequent visitor to his house. Often he listened to the two girls as they discussed music, art, and the French novels they were reading. Gradually, and without realizing it, he looked forward to Magda's visits. He didn't even mind her sarcasm when his French pronunciation amused her, as she took it upon herself to teach him the language.

The summer vacation presented him with other educational venues. He walked the streets of Cairo and became familiar with most of its lanes and alleys. He attended Sunday mass and Sunday school at a nearby Coptic church. But all the time he wondered about the mysteries he saw in the three religions he was familiar with, in the context of his relationship with Eva and its obscure future. He went to the open-air cinemas, which customarily showed two or three movies each evening. He visited most of the famous places in and around Cairo and learned more about their history. Sometimes Magda and Julia joined him, but most of the time he explored the city by himself.

David became especially enamored of the Nile. He saw it as a more beautiful and impressive body of water than the Suez Canal. He remembered the latter as a narrow channel hidden, at least in the vicinity of Kantara, between two sand banks in the middle of an arid desert. The Nile, however, was a wide majestic river surrounded by fertile, colorful fields. He felt a special intimacy with the Nile that kept him going to Road Al Farag, a riverboat terminal at the edge of Shoubra. There he took rides in a Felucca, the famous sailboat of the Nile, to see the rest of Cairo from that exhilarating vantage point. His first sighting of the Giza Pyramids happened during such a felucca ride and from that great distance. In the late 1940's, the pyramids were still visible on the horizon before the modern, tall, and crowded buildings blocked the view. A close-up look at the pyramids became a compelling obsession, which was finally gratified by his brother Joseph.

Early on one Friday, Joseph took him for his first visit to the pyramids. A tram ride delivered them to Ramsees Square, which became known as Tahrir

Square after the revolution of 1952. David was excited to see, in person, Kasr El Neil British Barracks, about which he had already heard from his history teacher. (It became the site of the Hilton Nile Hotel in later years.) Another tram took them across Kasr El Neil Bridge, through El Gezira Island, across another short bridge, and along Mourad Street to Giza Square, where the pyramids became more visible at the distance. One more tram took them through a short tunnel, and then along the whole length of the Pyramid Boulevard. Farms extended on each side of the boulevard, except in a few locations where Joseph pointed to the buildings of the Pyramid Cabaret on the right side and to the Villa of Fareeda, King Farouk's sister, on the left. No other buildings were in sight. That's before the agricultural land was appropriated for a new, haphazardly built residential district. The outline of the pyramids gradually enlarged into bigger and bigger dimensions until their colossal size filled the whole view, as the tram finally reached the foot of the pyramids' plateau.

The two brothers walked the steep, upward incline of a road that took them to the base of the great pyramid. David stood there in awe, overwhelmed by the enormity of the structure. However, his brother didn't give him a chance to digest the whole experience.

"Let's have a tour inside Khufu's pyramid before the sun gets too hot and the temperature inside would be intolerable," Joseph said, as he led his brother to the base of the great pyramid.

Joseph bought two tickets and helped his brother ascend the granite blocks on the northern face of the pyramid until they reached its entrance, some fifty-five feet above ground level. From there a downward slanting passageway was easy to negotiate until it joined the ascending corridor, where the two brothers had to bend down and literally crawl through its length. Fortunately, wooden crossbars, at reasonable distances on the floor of the steep tunnel, made their ascent more secure. The air inside was stagnant and stifling. Electric bulbs at regular intervals illuminated the way. With great effort and care, they managed to finally reach the spacious and corbelled-roofed Grand Gallery. With a sigh of relief, David stood up straight to take a deep breath and marvel at the majesty of that gallery. *How could his distant ancestors manage to build such a structure with its smooth granite walls and magnificent arched roof deep inside a massive pyramid?* David wondered, as the beauty of the space mesmerized him. He was tempted to linger there, but his brother urged him to ascend the last stretch to the king's chamber.

"That is it?" David asked in disbelief, as he entered the king's chamber.

"This empty room," Joseph said, "is the burial place of King Khufu."

David saw nothing in that room other than an undecorated granite sarcophagus; no mummy, no statues, no treasures, and no hieroglyphs on the walls. *What beliefs could have driven his ancestors to build such gigantic monuments just to preserve their dead bodies for eternity?* The question echoed in his head, again and again. When his bother told him about the ancient treasure-hunters who had robbed these tombs of their treasures and mummies, he felt sorry for the unfulfilled purpose of those massive buildings. Later generations of pharaohs must have found out that even those colossal pyramids didn't guarantee any protection to their mummies and treasures, nor did they give them the eternity they were looking for. *Maybe that explains why the pharaohs stopped building such pyramids after the Old Kingdom,* he reasoned.

Too many questions surged in David's mind. He wondered if the old Egyptian myths really differed from the present-day religious beliefs? If immortality were a fact, would a person repossess his own body, as the pharaohs believed, or would one go through eternity in a different state, in the spirit, as modern religions claimed?

Those questions gradually vanished as David exited the great pyramid and filled his lungs with fresh air. He was soon occupied with other thoughts, as he took a tour with his brother around the rest of the plateau to see the other two pyramids. The tour ended with a camel ride to the Sphinx.

David stood in front of the Sphinx, astonished by its size and beauty. When he saw its broken nose, he asked his brother about it.

"Napoleon did that," his brother said. "When the Mamelukes fought his army during the siege of Cairo, Napoleon aimed his guns at the Sphinx, in frustration and anger. I don't know if that's what happened, but this story is as good as any other to explain the damaged nose."

David thought it miraculous that the Sphinx, the pyramids, and all the other monuments of his country had survived the blunder of all the foreign invaders. He recalled his teacher's lessons when he had said that all invaders have come and gone, but Egypt endured.

The Friday after that, the two brothers went to Saqqara, the site of the Stepped Pyramid. A friend of Joseph, an archeologist in the antiquity's department, was waiting for them. He took them on a tour around the Saqqara complex and showed them the ruins that scattered all over the landscape, its walls and trenches. He guided them through the underground catacombs of the of Egle Abis tomb—the cow-god of Abis, one of the sacred deities of ancient Egypt. Finally, he circled with them around the Stepped Pyramid, the first monumental stone construction in the world. As they walked around, the archeologist told them about Imhotep, the master architect who designed and built that pyramid for King Zoser more than 2,600 years before Christ. He also explained how the idea of this pyramid came from its precursor, the one-step Mastaba, which was the original burial pit of previous pharaohs. The genius of Imhotep, he explained, was to conceive of building progressively smaller Mastabas on top of each other in a new, esthetically appealing pyramidal shape, constructed in stone. The history lesson ended when they were in the belly of the pyramid. The solemnity of the place and its awe-inspiring antiquity forced them to finish the tour in utter silence until they exited to the fading light of that day.

"You want to see a mummy?" Joseph's archeologist friend asked as he was saying his good-byes.

"Can I?" David asked with obvious eagerness.

The archeologist looked at his watch, and realizing that it was getting too late to see a darkened burial site, he promised to show them the mummy the following Friday.

The following Friday, the two brothers were on time for their appointment. Across from the Stepped Pyramid, the archeologist led them to a new dig site. Blocks of massive stones were recently placed on top of each other in an obvious attempt to recreate the entrance to an old tomb, like putting a jigsaw puzzle together. More stones, with numbers and coded markings, were still scattered around. The archeologist adjusted a large mirror across from that entrance as he led his guests into the tomb. At the end of what looked like a foyer, he adjusted another mirror opposite the first one, and the sunlight beamed down a descending corridor, which they gingerly negotiated by what appeared to be magically reflected sunlight. Finally, David found himself in what the archeologist described as the burial chamber, in which a completely preserved mummy, with sharp and well-defined features, lay in an open sarcophagus, lit only by the same reflected sunlight. A male organ clearly defined its gender.

As much as seeing one of his distant ancestors in person had overwhelmed him, David became more intrigued by what the archeologist pronounced after they were out in the open air. He told them that if he had enough funds, he would find more and more ruins under every inch of that desert. And David knew that he was telling them the truth.

David had to see another one of Cairo's landmarks on his own, as he had to visit it during a weekday to avoid the Friday's prayer that was bound to attract a large crowd to its mosque. That was the *Citadel,* the ancient fortress on top of the Mukattam Mountain, which was built by Salah El Dean El Ayoubi, the famous Saladin who drove the *Crusaders* out of the holy land. It was the same fortress that Mohammad Ali used for his quarters and built in it the magnificent mosque that carries his name. It was also the same fortress where Mohammad Ali had massacred the Mamelukes before he solidified his rule over Egypt.

David recalled all that history, which he had learned from his history teacher at the Kantara School, as he walked the winding road up the mountain. The house of Mohammad Ali, where the massacre took place, didn't impress him as much as the mosque. Not even his favorite Yafa's cathedral stood a chance if compared to that opulent mosque with its vast space and impressive, elaborately decorated dome. David sat down on the luxurious carpet exactly under the center of the dome, captivated by the beauty of the place and overwhelmed by its opulence. He became conscious of something greater than himself and felt an urge to pray, but he didn't know to whom he was supposed to pray—the Jewish Yahweh, the Christian God, or the Muslim Allah. Then he remembered Eva. He became certain of her transcendental presence, which gave him a legitimate claim to the three religions. Although it felt awkward to say a Christian prayer in a Muslim mosque, he finally, and silently, recited the Lord's Prayer. Then he exited the mosque.

A walk around the Citadel brought him to the wall that overlooked Cairo. The vast metropolis, seen from that vantage point, spread on both sides of the Nile, as the wide river streamed in its northerly course. The midtown area, dotted with ornate buildings and islands of public parks, looked like a vibrant oases in the middle of the desert. The whole scene reminded him of the story of Khedive Ismail. David found it necessary to give Ismail credit for the construction he added to this city, despite the fact that he was responsible for the British occupation of Egypt, as his teacher had taught. The magnificent Cairo he was looking at was the creation of that same Khedive, and he realized that there were always many sides to the same story.

The more he saw, the more he fell in love with the city. By the end of summer, he would have seen most of what was significant in and around Cairo. Finally, he considered himself to be a confident and a true Cairene. However, he did not forget Kantara, nor did he lose his affection for the only person he loved more than anybody else in the whole world—even when Magda became the object of his sexual fantasies.

AL KANATER AL KHAIREYA

"Tomorrow, I'll take you all to Al Kanater." Mr. Bishara announced the news to his family at dinner on a Thursday evening. "Joseph, you can bring your fiancé. Your uncle didn't object to that." He then looked at Julia and told her to bring Magda if she so desired. "The boat will leave from Road Al Farag at eight in the morning," he found it necessary to remind his children, "so be ready before that hour."

Al Kanater Al Khaireya is a vast public park, a few kilometers north of Cairo. It surrounds a strategic dam, Kanater, which straddles the Nile before it divides into its two main branches to enclose the Delta. The Kanater was built during the reign of Mohammad Ali, the founder of the modern Egyptian Dynasty.

David recalled the history of Mohammad Ali, the Albanian who came to Egypt in 1799 with the Turkish troops that, together with the British, unsuccessfully tried to drive the French out of Egypt after the Napoleonic invasion of the country. He recalled how Mohammad Ali remained in Egypt after the French armies were finally chased out of Alexandria, to ultimately become another one of the uninterrupted line of foreigners who ruled Egypt since Ptolemy's time. After the Ptolemies, Egypt was ruled by the Persians, the Romans, the Christians of Byzantium, and lastly, by the Arab Muslims with their successive dynasties until the last one, the Ottomans of Turkey and their surrogates, the Mamelukes.

Following the failure of the Napoleon's expedition in Egypt and the departure of the French army, Mohammad Ali managed to maneuver his way in the dangerous cast of the Mamelukes, who administered and ransacked Egypt in the name of the Ottomans. He finally became the most powerful Pasha outside the ranks of the Mamelukes.

Shortly thereafter, a British army landed in Alexandria to allegedly return the Mamelukes to power. After an initial and easy advance to Rosetta, the town where Napoleon archeologists had found the famous Rosetta Stone, Egyptian troops, led by Mohammad Ali, suddenly appeared from nowhere and massacred the invading force. The British had to retreat and to ultimately leave Egypt. That spectacular triumph solidified Mohammad Ali's command of the Egyptian forces. He was thus transformed from a foreign Albanian adventurer into a full-fledged Egyptian hero and the de facto governor of Egypt. To safeguard his rule, it became necessary for him to eliminate the Mamelukes.

The Mamelukes, or male slaves, who became a self-perpetuating cast, started to appear at the time of Salah Al Dean Al Ayoubi, the same Saladin who successfully fought the crusaders and founded the Ayyoubid dynasty in Egypt. Originally, the Mamelukes were young boys whom Saladin bought from the Caucasus, or Asia Minor, raised them in his court and indoctrinated them with Islamic teaching and blind loyalty to the Sultan. Their ascendancy became so dramatic that successive new generations of recruits ultimately deposed the Ayyoubid dynasty and ruled Egypt for six hundred years. When the Ottomans came to Egypt, they employed the Mamelukes as their surrogates and gave them a free mandate to exploit the country, as long as they paid taxes to the Ottoman Sultan in Istanbul.

Mohammad Ali dealt with the Mamelukes at what came to be known as the Citadel Massacre. He invited their leaders to a feast on a Friday afternoon at his quarters in Saladin's Citadel overlooking Cairo. After a lavish dinner at his palatial quarters, he withdrew with his entourage, leaving only the Mamelukes behind. Suddenly, his guards surrounded the Mamelukes and opened fire killing all of them, thus ending one dynasty to start another.

Despite all the atrocities he committed, history remembers Mohammad Ali as the great reformer and builder. At Al Kanater Al Khaireya, the dam that carries his name was considered one of his greatest achievements, second only to the Aswan Dam. The surrounding vast scenic park became the destination of the Cairenes when they wished to escape their crowded city, enjoy a walk on the body of the dam, lounge on the lush green grass, take a Felucca ride on the Nile, or just marvel at the magnificent river as it divided into its two terminal branches. This was the park that Mr. Bishara was talking about.

On the night of the promised outing, sleep eluded two people. In the case of Joseph, it was the prospect of being with his fiancé all day that kept him awake. Tradition prevented them from being together except in the presence of a chaperon, but he figured out that a large park would present ample opportunities to hide somewhere away from the watching eyes of his family. When he finally fell asleep, his fiancé was in his dreams, hugging and kissing him until he awoke ecstatic and fulfilled.

In the case of David, it was Eva who was on his mind. He wished that she, not Magda, would be the one to join them in that outing. He didn't have anything against Magda, but he felt vulnerable in her presence, which gave him a feeling of unfaithfulness to Eva. Ultimately both girls were on his mind when he fell asleep. When he woke at dawn, a gripping sense of guilt overwhelmed him when he realized that Eva wasn't the partner in his dreams. It was Magda.

Early on Friday, Joseph brought his fiancé, and Magda came to the house. The mother filled a basket with food and drinks. After a short tram ride to Road El-Farag, Mr. Bishara's entourage walked to the pier where the father paid for the tickets, and all of them rushed to the upper deck of the ferry. Soon the boat was on its way to Al Kanater Al Khaireya.

Mr. Bishara's company took its place on board and joined the rest of the passengers to watch the ferry as it departed from the pier and found its way to the middle of the river, where it took a steady course to the north. The rhythmic clicking of the steam engine gradually became a comforting beat of progression, rather than the annoying and disturbing noise it was. The dark, smoky column that trailed from the bellowing chimney and the whitish foamy waters that the boat left behind as it cut its way on the surface of the river seemed to join in the execution of an abstract painting. Across the distant shores, small villages and farms appeared to hug the Nile, as if in gratitude to the life-giving river. The magical beauty of the Nile is nowhere more apparent or more impressive than when one is a passenger on a ship floating in the middle of its stream.

When the ferry steadied in its course, everyone on board became engaged in talking and yelling and laughing at the same time. The ensuing blithe chatter soon enough masked the din of the boat's engine. The resulting clatter would have been irritating in a confined space like the one of that boat, or in the surrounding peaceful scenery. However, nobody seemed to be bothered by the noise or interested in the scenery. Egyptians traditionally take life for granted, as if the river, the fertile land, the mild weather, and even their country's rich history seem to give them such a fatalistic feeling of permanency that they treat the wealth of their country with unconscionable indifference. They converse in loud voices and animated gestures that you would think they were fighting. They open their radios to the loudest volume. They throw their garbage in the streets and in their river and canals. And they show generosity beyond their capabilities or means and offer their hospitality to friends and enemies alike.

All that noise subsided when a small musical band of students started to play. The instruments included an Ood, a large bulky mandolin-like instrument, a violin, and a drum. After the opening piece of music, a performer stood in front of the band, singing and telling jokes. Most of the passengers joined in the singing, when they recognized one of the popular songs, or shared in a hearty laughter at the jokes. This festive ritual lasted until the boat reached its destination at Al Kanater Al Khaireya.

Mr. Bishara took his company to a grassy knoll where a mimosa tree, with its branches spreading like an overhanging umbrella, covered the underlying grass with a cooling shade. An abundance of pink flowers adorned the mimosa tree, and multicolored pansies were densely arranged in nearby flowerbeds. Scents of jasmine and gardenia wafted in the air. As the sun ascended along its trajectory, the air felt warmer, but a gentle breeze, blowing from the river's direction, tempered that. Mr. Bishara rested his back on the tree trunk and closed his eyes, as if to give permission to the rest of his company to do as they pleased. However, everyone stayed at the spot, enchanted by the beauty of the surrounding nature. At lunchtime, the mother spread the contents of her basket and offered each one a share from the sandwiches, fruits, and drinks. In the early afternoon, the same jasmine-scented breeze filled the younger people with sensual energy that they had no way to release, except in a game of racket ball. The parents were content with a card game.

After an exhausting racket-ball game in the sun, Joseph suggested a row-boat excursion on the river. The parents declined his invitation and gave their permission for the rest to go.

"I'll start the rowing." Joseph said when his company was seated in the rowboat. When they reached the open waters, he handed the oars to David.

"Here, David," Joseph said. "Give it a try."

The boat started to rock precariously when the two brothers stood up to exchange their seats. Magda had to stand up to allow extra room for that exchange. She had to hold onto David to steady herself. The three girls were screaming and laughing until the two men settled down in their respective places. During that commotion, David took Magda's embrace for what it appeared to be, an innocent and unintentional contact of their bodies. But when he grasped the paddles, he found himself overcome by pleasure, the same sensation he had experienced when Magda was in his dreams the previous night. Quickly, he regained his composure and started to row, but his mind was busy with something else. Did she intentionally embrace him? Was she really afraid or just pretending to be? He knew that he was a few years younger than she; he couldn't have possibly interested her. Before he could reach a conclusion, a shower of water from his inexperienced rowing splashed onto his face and brought him back to reality. Everybody else was getting wet, too. Although Joseph was enjoying the feeling of the wet, soft body of his fiancé, he was compelled to take control of the boat himself. Another episode of rocking, screaming, laughing, hand holding, and body pressing followed until the boat settled down into a manageable pace. This time around, David convinced himself that Magda did not only squeeze his body, but also seemed to enjoy it.

Back under the mimosa tree, their father was taking a nap. David joined his mother in a card game, while Joseph took his fiancé for a walk. The other two girls sat on the body of the dam, not far away. David's mind wasn't totally concentrating on the card game. His mother prevailed in one game after another, while he was floating in a dream-like state thinking of Eva and wondering about the meaning of the pleasurable sensation he experienced when Magda had held to him during the boat ride. A sense of betrayal overwhelmed him when he remembered his love and commitment to Eva. Ultimately, Eva's presence dominated all his thoughts and eliminated everything else.

The return trip was a repeat of the morning one, except for the sunset. By then the temperature had cooled, and the air became permeated with the numbing smells of the Egyptian countryside—a mixture of cut alfalfa, cow manure, and burning hay. The stage was thus set for the display of colors left behind on the western horizon by the setting sun. Scattered clouds added definition to the diverging rays, and the fading blue of the skies formed a background of reddish hues. David was deeply engrossed in that beauty when he suddenly felt something pressing against his body. Magda was sitting next to him, touching his body. If there was an initial doubt about her intentions, it disappeared when a tight grip from her hand transmitted an unmistakable desire and a clear message that made the blood rush into his sensitive body and awaken the same feelings he had experienced in his dream. But suddenly, before he had enough time to enjoy her touch, she withdrew to another corner of the boat, as if she intended to take him to the cliff and leave him there to jump or rescue himself. Afraid that somebody might have witnessed that fast exchange, he had no choice but to rescue himself. He concentrated his attention on the sunset until he gradually felt his blood returning to its normal flow. When they left the boat at Road Al Farag, Magda walked away with his sister and never looked at him again, as if nothing had happened.

From that day on, David became aware of a dramatic change; he had developed an attachment to another girl. *But that attachment was like a fantasy or a dream, nothing real,* he reassured himself. And fantasies could be the only escape in a segregated society. He thus would allow himself to fantasize as much as he wanted as long as he remained faithful to his Eva. That's it: his dream about Magda wasn't a betrayal. The embrace wasn't a sin, and he didn't initiate the sunset incident. It wasn't until a year later that his instincts overcame his reason. And his instincts took over.

THE VIOLIN

The first year in high school opened a new chapter in David's life, more exciting and more challenging than he had ever imagined. His initial insecurity and shaky confidence soon gave way to a more assured attitude, once he saw his academic level to be on par with that of the other students. The summer vacation had also prepared him for the tougher character of his new colleagues. As his school was all-boys one—all schools in Egypt were segregated by sex; the Kantara one represented an exception. In these segregated schools, the teenage students were more vulgar in their language and rougher in their behavior. The society they lived in made them express their suppressed sexual desires in fantasies, dreams, and foul language, which were, in fact, not foreign to David. However, his love for Eva made him refrain from the street language and sublimate his desires to a more worthy goal. And for her sake, he became more determined to excel in his studies, finish high school with good grades, enter medical school, and become a great doctor. And, for his own good fortune, two influential persons determined his subsequent development.

The first one was Salama Mousa, a revolutionary Egyptian thinker who was educated in Europe and who took it upon himself to familiarize the younger generations with the knowledge and culture of the *Western civilization*. Mousa was a Renaissance intellectual who believed in the importance of studying all branches of knowledge. His column in the daily newspaper, "Akhbar Al Youm," and his books opened a new world to the readers who were willing to receive his message. David became one of his disciples. Through the writings of Salama Mousa, David acquired a fascination for knowledge and inquiry and channeled his readings into a more critical and purposeful direction that put him on the road to become the intellectual Salama Mousa was calling for.

The second person was his mother, who had already introduced him to the magical world of music. Faithful to her promise, she bought him a violin when he graduated from the primary school with honors, and she taught him the basic language of music. The school's music teacher took care of the rest.

As the academic year progressed, the war in Palestine came to an end in January of 1949 with the defeat of the Arab armies and the signing of a cease-fire truce between Egypt and Israel. When it became known that Israel had besieged the elite Fallujah unit of the Egyptian army, the Egyptians became bitterly demoralized. A popular uproar swept the streets of Cairo, as the military blamed the defeat on defective weapons. It was claimed that some of the king's cronies had profited by conspiring with dishonest European dealers to supply the Egyptian army with faulty weapons. Nobody in power escaped the wrath of the angry masses that directed their revolutionary fervor against the king, all the political parties, and above all, against the British. Vocal demonstrators marched from all corners of the city and headed to Cairo University, as the students took a leading role in the demand for reform.

It wasn't unusual for high school students to cut their classes, take the tram to the university, and join other high school and university students in big demonstrations, as if hidden strings were moving them in a previously rehearsed show. A few regular speakers took control of the crowds and directed their energies against some enemy or another, depending on the particular occasion of that day. After some poetic speeches, the entire body of students would march through the streets and head to the British embassy, the king's palace, or the house of parliament, as that specific day's issue demanded, to shout the appropriate slogans for each of the above destinations.

David's first demonstration was a novel experience. One of the senior students took charge of the school and gathered all the students in the school courtyard. He had an imposing figure, a deep voice, and a good command of the language. The school's administrators didn't question his intent or try to stop him, as if his power had come from a higher authority. After a brief speech, he led the willing students out of the school gate, commandeered a tram, and instructed the conductor to drive to the university.

David sat in the streetcar contemplating different thoughts as the tram screeched its way through the busy streets of Cairo. He discovered, to his delight, that the demonstrators didn't have to pay for the ride. More than that, he found out that the students effectively owned the tram for that day. They could run it, stop it, and take it to wherever they wanted. They even seemed to own the whole city, as people in the streets stopped and clapped and repeated the same slogans after the screaming demonstrators.

Cairo University occupied a prime area in Giza, the twin city of Cairo west of the Nile. A high fence surrounded the whole campus, and a wide, beautifully landscaped street led to the Nile from its impressive front gate. The Giza Zoo bordered it on one side and the Orman Garden on the other. The entrance opened into a wide courtyard, at the end of which stood the elevated main building with its wide steps, imposing columns, and impressive dome. Separate buildings, with matching architectural design, housed the different faculties or schools, and grassy lawns scattered in the empty spaces between them. Ornamental trees in strategic locations completed the picture. All faculties were housed in that complex except for two: the Faculty of Engineering, which was across the street, and the Faculty of Medicine, which was at the Cairo side of the river.

The university students were already gathered in front of the main building when David's group arrived. More high school students came from different directions, and the university courtyard filled to capacity with screaming demonstrators. Speeches were already in progress, and David stood there impressed by the eloquence of the speakers. Some of them recited poetry, some spoke in colloquial verse, and others in just plain Arabic. But all of them attacked the ruling party and called for the election of the Wafd party, the dominant and most popular party in the country that was in the opposition at that time.

A long procession followed, as everyone marched behind the leaders of the demonstration. From the University Street, they turned left on Mourad Street in Giza then crossed the Nile on Kasr El Neil Bridge to Ismailia Square in Cairo. Fully armed police officers blocked the roads that led to the British Embassy, which was in Garden City, the exclusive district of Cairo to the east of the river just south of the square. However, on that particular day, the parliament, which was located a few blocks from there, was their final destination. More speeches and yelling followed until everybody was exhausted. If anything was accomplished, nobody knew about it. However, everybody was content with the whole exercise, as the demonstrators disbursed and each one went his own separate way.

During the rest of that school year, other events presented different reasons for more demonstrations. In the end, the king had to dissolve the parliament and call for new elections.

The political campaign was something new for David. By then he had become a true patriot and a revolutionary, influenced, no doubt, by the lessons of his history teacher at Kantara School. His sympathies were with the Wafd Party, the majority party that represented the common people. It was customary at that time to erect huge tents of intricately and colorfully designed thick fabric in the streets of Cairo, where people would congregate and listen to the campaign speakers. The political process appeared to be truly democratic; anyone could run for office and everyone could speak his mind. But the elections were mostly fraudulent; money, fame, or political connections usually decided the winners. Well-renowned speakers, mostly lawyers or students in the faculty of law, made their rounds in these tents. Without exception, all of them had a unique mastery of the Arabic language and used it expertly for their desired goals.

David rarely failed to attend these political rallies whenever he saw one of those colorful tents. He became fascinated with the Arabic language as he continued to listen to these speakers. He even wrote a long poem and recited it in front of one of those rallies. It started as follows:

My father told me, come you on,

Come forth, my son, my country's own.

Mine years were wasted in mine fight,

Mine hair turned gray and thin and light.

Now it's up to you, to your generation,

To end the suffering, the humiliation,

And avenge me from my evil occupier,

And rid the country of a despotic ruler.

The Wafd Party won the election and formed a new government. As an optimistic mood prevailed, the students went back to their schools without any further interruptions or distractions. The final exam put David at the top of his class, and he was ready to see Eva. But this had to wait until his mother arranged a trip to Kantara. In the meantime, he used all his energy and time to practice his violin. A more competent teacher than the one at school became necessary, and his mother arranged for one.

The Cairenes like to say that "Egypt is the mother of the world, and Cairo is its center." Ethnic groups from all corners of the world made Cairo their home and infused the local culture with their own until the city acquired its special cosmopolitan character. The French put their mark on the architecture of the city. The Italians brought their statues and music. The Germans taught their engineering skills and discipline. The Greeks ran the restaurants and liquor stores. The Lebanese came with their beautiful women, talented writers, and famous actors and singers. The British, more than anybody else, spread their language and traditions. At that time, few of the world's capitals could have matched Cairo in its weather, vibrancy, opportunities, and rich cultural life.

An Italian institute for music was a premier school in downtown Cairo. Its Italian teachers performed with the Cairo Symphony Orchestra and taught at the institute. That's where David's mother wanted him to go.

"It is time for you to start your classical training," she said.

One hour of instruction a week was supplemented by a few hours of practice every day, and David started his musical journey to become a classical violin player.

Inevitably, the end of the school year brought him closer to Magda, as she was a constant companion to his sister. It was natural for him to join the two girls, whether they met in his house or in hers. He also joined them in their evening stroll in Shoubra Street, where they customarily bought sunflower seeds, grilled corn on the cob, or cactus fruit. The two girls insisted on conversing in French, even in his presence. At first he had to manage with the few words he learned at school, but he put greater effort into expanding his vocabulary until he became able to make decent conversations in French.

Music wasn't Magda's priority, though she played the piano well. Painting was. She filled her house with her colorful paintings, and it was no secret that she was going to join the Faculty of Fine Arts at Cairo University.

Magda, a couple of years older than David, was endowed with a well-proportioned, sensual body. She was aware of her effect on the opposite sex early on, as men followed her in the street with looks and comments suggestive of desire and admiration. But in a conservative society, there was nothing much a girl like her could do to satisfy her instinctive needs. Worse still, attending a Catholic school reinforced an even stricter morality. Reward or punishment hovered over all behavior, as good and evil became more defined. Suppressed urges had no release, except to be transferred to a worthy cause or person, in the best of circumstances—or vulgarities, in the worst. Magda, like some of the girls in her school, idolized one of the nuns and made her the target of her love. Therefore it became inevitable that at some time in her adolescent years, that she decided to become a nun. Gradually, however, the romantic French novels that she read excited her imagination and made her reconsider her decision. But how could she relive the experience of her French heroines if her society denied her the freedom they appeared to enjoy?

The arrival of David changed everything. Initially, he didn't seem to resemble any of the characters in her French novels, and the difference in their age was obvious. As she usually spent most of her time with his sister, there was no possibility of ignoring David's constant presence. Gradually, the three of them became regular companions without any fear of breaking the traditional conservative rules, as it was socially acceptable for them to be together. However, his presence inevitably started to awaken her suppressed sensuality—the same sensuality she found in the French novels—until it expressed itself during the Kanater trip. For the first time in her life, a man's touch brought to life the things she had only read about. Pleasure wasn't fiction anymore; it was real. When she first held to him during the rowboat incident, she didn't know what to make of her feelings. She tried to explore it further when she held his hand and pressed her body against his in the ferry. There was no doubt in her mind—she was a woman with feelings and desires. From that day on, she saw David in a different light, especially when he went through a growth spurt that year. He had awakened her sensuality, and more assuredly, he was also there at a safe distance and in a socially acceptable environment. There would be no risk in seeing him, as long as she was willing to go as far as she could to enjoy that mysterious feeling, but not far enough to risk a scandal or, worse still, her virginity. As the school year progressed, their studies kept them apart, except for occasional encounters. However, her desires became more pressing on the arrival of spring and the summer vacation.

So it happened that one day, she saw his mother and sister leaving the house. She knew that he would be alone, and she couldn't resist anymore.

"Where is Julia?" She asked in an innocent voice when he opened the door. She was already in the living room when he said that his sister and mother had gone out.

"I see that you are holding your violin. Did I take you away from your practice?" She asked.

"Oh, no," he said, as he felt an urge to keep her around. "Actually, I have been practicing all morning, and my fingers are getting tired."

"I know what you mean," she said in a similar attempt to extend the visit. "My fingers too get tired when I play too much on the piano. Can I try your violin?"

"Of course," he answered, as he handed her the violin. She tried to play it, but only discordant sounds came out.

"Would you show me how to hold it?" She asked in an innocent but seductive voice.

He went behind her to show her the correct position. She felt his body close to hers, and she instinctively started to rub against him until she felt his erection. When she bent down to put the violin aside, he grasped her buttocks in his hands and started rubbing against them.

She straightened up and turned around. Armed with theoretical knowledge from her French novels, she said, "Let's do it the right way."

She opened her mouth to receive his tongue and sucked it deep into her throat. She then let go of his tongue and extended her own into his mouth to give him the same experience.

"You know how to kiss," she said, after she managed to get her tongue back. "When did you learn that?"

He wasn't in a state to answer. He pressed her mouth against his and felt for her tongue again. Gradually, her mouth descended along his neck and down his chest and abdomen until it ended between his thighs. She pulled down his pants, and then ran her face along his erect penis until it ended in her mouth. When he finally ejaculated, she stretched her body on the floor and pulled him on top of her.

"Just be careful," she said when he pulled down her underwear. "You have to do it from the outside." Obediently, he exposed her thighs and moved up and down until he felt her tense body relaxing under him at the same time he ejaculated on her thighs.

"This is wonderful," she said. She was tempted to keep him on top of her, but the wet feeling made her push him away and stand up. She wiped her thighs, pulled up her underwear, straightened her dress, and ran out of the apartment.

When circumstances didn't present them with occasions to be alone, it wasn't too difficult for her to convince the two families to let them practice music together. The age difference made remote any suspicion of their motive. And they kept practicing their music. When her mother was in the house, they did just that. But when the mother wasn't there, they practiced something else. However, Magda was always in control and knew how and when they must stop. She knew how to satisfy herself but only to the limit that preserved her virginity.

It wasn't that David had forgotten Eva that made him seek those stolen encounters with Magda. He was certain that his love for Eva would endure, despite that apparent infidelity. *Sexual gratification,* he convinced himself, *was the only thing that attracted him to Magda, and he suspected that she felt the same way.* After all, he was sure that a man of her age would ultimately get her full attention and take her away from him. Fortunately, he didn't have to endure this conflict for long. In Kantara, his sister was due to have a new baby, and their mother agreed to go and take him with her to Kantara.

THE RETURN TO KANTARA

As the train sped out of Cairo and the distance between him and Magda increased, it became easier for David to detach himself from his obsession with her. The detachment became complete as the sights and smells of Kantara brought vivid images of Eva. He knew that he wasn't as innocent as when he had left her more than a year earlier. *But his sins, he reasoned, were those of the flesh, not of the soul.* He was determined to be deserving of her love and to find a way to overcome their religious differences. He still thought maybe they could escape to a distant country where nobody would object to their marriage. His experiences in the past year in Cairo had brought him in contact with different people and cultures, which convinced him that there was a big world out there. In that world people were free to believe in whatever they wanted, without any restrictions from religious fanaticism or fake moralism. Yes, escaping to a foreign country would be their salvation. He was comforted by the fact that one year was already behind him. Four more years and Eva would go to Cairo to attend the university. She only had to remain free until then.

As he labored to find a way to see Eva, his mother made his job easy; she took him with her when she visited Eva's family. He felt his heart pounding in his chest when Eva came to the room. A full year had added more growth, more beauty, and more maturity to her appearance. For a moment, he wondered if she still loved him. A firm yet tender handshake dissipated his fears. He looked into her eyes, and the message was clear. Time didn't change her. She was undoubtedly his.

"Look at these two beautiful children," David's mother said.

"They are not children anymore," Eva's mother said. She then addressed David, "I am glad you're in Cairo now," she told him. And as if to hide her true and hidden meaning, she quickly added, "They have better schools there."

"Yes, aunt."

"How did you do in school?" Again, she directed her question to David, but his mother volunteered the answer.

"He was at the top of his class. How about Eva?"

"She was at the top too," Eva's mother answered proudly. Then she added, "Eva has been studying very hard, so we would let her finish her education and go to the university. This is nonsense. A girl should get married as soon as she is of age."

Nothing of this sort should be allowed to happen, David thought. *Eva had to remain free until they were able to escape to a free country as he had previously planned. Could he depend on Eva to remain free? There was only one way to know for sure; they must meet in the cemetery like in the good old days.* A stolen look and a meaningful nod was all he could manage to let her know his thoughts, and she appeared to understand his signals.

The evening after, he found himself walking to their favorite spot in the British cemetery. Unsure if she had understood his hints, he waited and waited, but she didn't show up. For five evenings he returned to the cemetery in the hope that she might ultimately come. On his sixth attempt, she did.

"Eva!" he shouted. "I knew you would eventually show up. I have been coming here for the last five days."

"I know," she said.

He didn't wait for further explanation, as he blocked her open mouth with his and held her in his arms. When, after a few minutes, she managed to release her lips from his, she didn't feel a need to speak. She let him press against her body, as she started to shake in apparent ecstasy, until she relaxed in a blissful contentment.

"I love you, David," she said. "You have always been with me, but this is different. This feels more real and exhilarating than when you visited me in my dreams."

"I know, Eva. I have been having the same dreams. You're right. This is different."

A guilty feeling tormented him for a moment as Magda's naked body flashed in his mind. Strangely enough, he couldn't recall the details of Magda's features. He wondered if sex without love made her faceless in his mind. This must be true, for he recalled how much he thought he loved Magda during each of their sexual encounters but not in between, not in the same way he felt about Eva. *Love makes it different,* he concluded. He stopped himself from saying anything further lest he betrayed his own thoughts. No further explanation was needed anyway.

"Your mother wasn't serious in what she had said about marriage, was she?" he asked, as he looked at Eva's face with an inquisitive intensity.

"I don't know why she said that." Eva said. "My mother used to be the one who wanted me to go to the university, not my father. Lately, they have reversed their positions. She seems like she wants to get rid of me, when my father is encouraging me to postpone marriage until I completed my studies. 'You know, Eva,' my father often tells me, 'I look at you as the son I never had. You are even better than a son. You are a smart, hard-working girl. As long as you keep up your grades, I'll let you go to the university. Don't worry about your mother; she will come around.' So, don't worry, David. I am doing very well at school, and I am sure they will send me to the university."

He wanted to believe her. Lingering doubts quickly disappeared, as he felt an urge to embrace her again, but she slipped away from his arms.

"I can't stay out for long," she said. "My parents have become stricter since I went to high school…"

"I don't blame them," he interrupted her. "You have grown up in the last year. I can understand their reasons. A lot of men are probably attracted to you."

"That's what worries them, especially my mother. I guess that's why she wants me to marry as soon as possible. They have become very protective of me, as if some man would steal me if they lowered their guard. Just now I had to lie to get permission to go out. 'I am going to visit my girlfriend,' I told them. I have to go before they look for me in her house. I shouldn't stay any longer, David. Good-bye for now."

"Are we going to see each other again?" he shouted after her.

"I don't know, David. But I'll try."

Whether she tried or not, he had no way of knowing. He didn't see her again during his stay in Kantara. When he inquired about her family, he discovered that they had left town to visit some relatives.

He walked around her house everyday looking for any sign of her return. He even knocked on the door to make sure that nobody was hiding inside. He went to the cemetery to console himself by recalling memories of their previous encounters. He practiced on his violin and read his books for hours just to kill time waiting for her return.

But Eva didn't return. He went back to Cairo without seeing her. In fact he didn't see her for the next four years, although he returned to Kantara during every summer vacation. Each time he returned, he would find out that her mother had taken her away to visit her Jewish family. Four years were too much for him to bear, but he had no choice but to endure the remainder of her high school years. Then Eva would supposedly, and hopefully, go to Cairo. On the occasions that he feared she might not go to the university or even that she might be forced to marry someone else, he would fall victim to despondency and depression. It was only through his friend Hassan that he kept track of Eva. And through Hassan, David knew that Eva didn't get married and that she was indeed going to the university.

THE BLACK
SATURDAY

Although the speed of time is always constant, the perception of its passage, whether slow or fast, is completely subjective. To David, waiting for the high school years to end and for Eva to come to Cairo might have felt like an eternity. However, he was involved with many things that made the passage of time more tolerable. His extra-curricular reading broadened his knowledge and helped him finish his homework quickly. With extra free time on his hand, he managed to pursue other activities and hobbies as well. He continued his violin lessons, read more and more books, explored the history of his country through visits to the extraordinary monuments left behind by his recent and distant ancestors, and participated in the political turmoil that followed the defeat in Palestine. Another spurt of physical growth propelled him into an early adulthood, and he was already well developed at the age of seventeen. On top of all this, his secretive affair with Magda added more self-confidence, maturity, and polish to his character. True, Magda started as a mentor guiding him through sexual and intellectual development, but he quickly gained an equal footing with her to form a symbiotic partnership.

Together, but mostly in the company of Julia, they listened to music, went to the movies, read and discussed books, walked in the parks, visited museums, and challenged each other's intellect. And when Julia wasn't around and circumstances permitted, they enjoyed stolen moments of sensual intimacy. If they couldn't be alone in either one of their homes as often as they wanted, they managed to meet in isolated areas, such as the desert of Heliopolis or the hills around the pyramids. With careful scheming and maneuvering, they eluded the discovery of their liaisons. Even Julia didn't suspect their secret affair.

Magda graduated from high school two years ahead of David, and as expected, she enrolled in the Faculty of Fine Arts at Cairo University to pursue her artistic studies. Suddenly she found herself in a completely new environment, free to come and go and free to consort with the other sex, unhindered by the watching eyes of her parents and neighbors. However, she didn't exploit her new freedom. Although her good looks, self-confidence, and mastery of several languages made her stand out among the female students, she didn't rush into the mating game like the rest of them. She didn't have to; David, with his precocious maturity, satisfied her desires and instinctive needs. In addition, her newly found freedom as a university student gave her more opportunity than before for safer encounters with David, which conveniently happened because of the increasing numbers of demonstrations that brought him often to the university.

During his last two years in high school, David became one of the youngest revolutionary leaders of the student movement. A command of the Arabic language and a talent for public speaking in rhyming verse complimented an imposingly tall and well-built body to propel him into the inner circle of the students' leadership. Ridding the country of the British occupation was the rallying cry for the revolutionary students. Each political party of that time had its own ideological agenda that dictated the direction of the power struggle for the control of the government. As the students were the largest and the most-opinionated group to be involved in politics, each party recruited as many students as it could. The big winner was the Wafd Party. A succession of nationalistic leaders, with their heroic struggles against the British occupation, the corrupted monarchy, the idle aristocrats, and the feudal lords had attracted the majority of Egyptians to the Wafd Party. It didn't make any difference that the latest leaders of the party had become less heroic and more corrupted, the party itself never lost its appeal. Somehow, its leaders managed to embrace popular patriotic and social issues that didn't fail to galvanize the populace. Back in 1936, they managed to extract a treaty from the British to limit the occupation forces to the Suez Canal Zone. Although their gains from that treaty evaporated years later when they rode to power on the tanks of the British against the will of the popular king and the sentiment of the people, the alternative parties were so opportunistic and corrupted that the Wafdists soon regained their popularity. By 1951 they were back in power. They implemented revolutionary reforms in education, health care, and many other social programs that propelled them to a dominant position, far ahead of any other party. From this position of strength, they dared to abrogate the 1936 treaty and demanded the evacuation of all the occupying British forces from the Canal Zone, ushering in fast-changing events that catapulted the country into a turbulent era.

Momentous events that change the course of history don't happen by accident. They have to be properly understood in the perspective of the cause-and-effect sequence of events that lead to them. As a history student, David thought that he had an educated grasp on what was happening in his country, but like everybody else, he couldn't have foreseen the events of January 1952.

When the Wafdist government unilaterally abrogated the 1936 treaty in October, 1951, it didn't declare or conduct a formal war. However, the extremist elements of the population—the Muslim Brotherhood, the Communists, and the Socialists—executed an insurgency war against the British forces. They attacked a munitions depot at Tel el Kebir, near Ismailia, which gave the British an opportunity to retaliate against the Egyptian government. The British incriminated an Egyptian auxiliary police unit for that attack and surrounded the police force at Ismailia. They gave them an ultimatum to hand in their arms and surrender. When the police unit refused to comply with the humiliating demands of the ultimatum, the British attacked their station on January 25, 1952, and erased it to the ground. By the end of the day, forty-six auxiliaries were dead, and over one hundred were wounded. A wave of anger and revolt against the British and everything foreign swept the country and ended in the "Black Saturday" of January 26, 1952.

David went early to school on that day in anticipation of another demonstration. He joined his fellow revolutionaries as they gathered to plan the course of action. Soon, the students poured out of the classrooms into the school courtyard waiting for directions from their leaders. David took his assigned role and started on one of his inflammatory speeches, until the emotions of his listeners were sufficiently aroused to start the march to the university.

As usual, he delivered his contingent to the university grounds. There was nothing more for him to do except to take his position among the crowd and listen to the older and more experienced leaders; his high school credentials didn't entitle him to compete in such a large and formidable forum. He thus decided to seek Magda, as was his habit during previous demonstrations.

On entering the cafeteria of the Faculty of Fine Arts, he saw Magda sitting with a male student. She was holding her companion's hand and appeared to be engrossed in an intimate conversation with him. Until that moment, David had taken his relationship with Magda for granted. He didn't see the difference in their ages as a problem. He also dismissed the possibility that men of her age might seek her love and affection. He stood there motionless, as if paralyzed, a victim of conflicting impulses. An initial feeling of jealousy was driving him to proceed and make his presence known. However, the harsh reality quickly immobilized him in his place, as if a mask was suddenly lifted off from his eyes. Magda was older than he was, and he had to admit she had the right to see older men. *At any event,* he reasoned, *they would have to break their relationship the following year, when Eva would come to Cairo.* With a heavy heart, he quietly withdrew and returned to the demonstration. But the image of Magda holding the hand of her companion stayed vivid in his mind until more momentous events eventually demanded all his attention.

The speeches were winding down by the time he returned. He joined the demonstrators as the procession crossed the river on its way to the prime minister's office to show support for the government and to condemn the brutality of the British forces. More slogans were shouted, and more speeches were delivered until a representative of the prime minister showed up in the balcony of his office. He acknowledged the demonstrators and reassured them that their government was relentlessly working to respond to the British murderous attack in Ismailia and get rid of the occupation, once and for all. David figured out that his job was done, as the demonstration was approaching its end. Expecting nothing more to happen, he aimlessly walked away until he found himself in the Opera Square.

The Opera Square, in Cairo's midtown area, was especially designed to showcase the Cairo Opera House. A cinema and a cabaret stood to one side of the square, and the expansive Azbakeya Park, the central park of Cairo, bordered it on the other side. A low stone fence and a wide pedestrian walkway separated the park from the square and was a renowned market for used books, arts, and crafts that attracted buyers of limited budgets, especially students and young intellectuals.

David was browsing through the second-hand books that crowded the fence of Azbakeya when a commotion at the other corner of the square drew his attention. When he reached the site of that commotion, he found out that a fight had started in front of Badee'a Massabny's Cabaret. In the middle of the screaming and yelling, he gathered the information that a police officer was drinking with one of the cabaret's hostesses. Someone had objected to the officer's unacceptable, immoral behavior when his comrades were being killed in Ismailia. A fight ensued that drew the angry crowds. David was about to enter the place, when screaming mobs, fleeing from an expanding fire, drove him back. In no time, the whole place was ablaze. After a short while, the same mob set fire to the adjoining cinema. An ever-increasing crowd filled the square and overflowed in steady streams to all corners of the midtown area. A sickening feeling of an impending calamity filled David with fear that he thought it prudent to return home.

His route to Shoubra took him through Ibrahim Pasha Street. Again he met screaming and angry mobs in front of the famous Shepheard Hotel, where foreign dignitaries and wealthy tourists habitually stayed. He reached the place in time to witness this symbol of foreign dominance go down in flames. A few blocks farther, he saw a foreign car dealership broken into—its cars pushed out and burned. The whole place was then set on fire.

He gradually became convinced that these incidents were not isolated ones but appeared to be simultaneously carried out by well-organized acts of revenge, though nothing was mentioned about any burning plans in his meetings with the students' organizational committees. Oblivious to his own safety, he roamed the streets of Cairo, where he saw detachments of angry mobs systematically setting fires to many foreign institutions, especially the British and Jewish ones. He saw trucks, carrying men and petrol, patrolling the streets of the midtown area and setting fires in cinemas, bars, cabarets, foreign clubs, and hotels without any obvious government interference. It was only before dusk that he saw soldiers appear in the streets to stop the carnage and prevent the rest of Cairo from burning into ashes.

The burning stopped as suddenly as it had started, but not before another destructive force had taken over—the inevitable looting. Gridiron gates, metal bars, and massive locks didn't prevent looters from breaking into stores and businesses. They carried out whatever items they could, and then they destroyed the rest.

It was already dark when David decided that he had seen enough. His beloved Cairo was burned, ransacked, and destroyed, and he couldn't do anything about it. As if he had suddenly awakened from a nightmare, he realized how late it was. His family must have been worried about him. With tears in his eyes and a heavy heart pounding in his chest, he walked back to his house.

"Thank God you're safe," his mother said, as she took him in her arms when he entered the house.

"Where have you been all day?" his father asked. "I hope that you didn't participate in the burning."

"No," he answered.

"Then where were you all day?" his father repeated.

"In the morning," he started to explain, "I led my school demonstrators to the university. You all know that I have been taking a leading part at our school, and you, father, didn't object to that. I walked with the demonstrators to the prime minister's office, and then I went downtown to look at the used books at the Azbakeya Park." He showed them the books he had bought, before he continued. "I was at the Opera Square when they started burning the cabaret and cinema opera. I didn't want to be part of it, so I decided to come home."

"How come it took you the whole day to reach home?" his father asked.

He described to them all the events he had witnessed. He ended up by saying, "I can't explain my behavior. I don't know why I couldn't detach myself from those events or why I stayed in the streets of Cairo when the burning and the destruction were going on. It seemed as if I were sleepwalking or experiencing a dreadful dream."

"That's fine, David." His mother had to end the interrogation. "It is enough that you are safely back at home. All is well that ends well. For us it was a scare. I hope that it was a lifetime learning experience for you. I don't blame you for staying in the city all that time. It is a rare experience for anyone to see a city go up in flame. I am sure that your experience will stay with you all your life, for good or for bad."

She was right. The memory of the burning of Cairo stayed with him, but it didn't prepare him, or anyone else, for the succeeding events of that year.

THE SUNDAY AFTER

S undays were special days for the Bishara family. Every Sunday, the extended family, including most of its members who lived in the big city, converged on Shoubra to attend the morning mass in a neighboring Coptic Church, after which they congregated in the Bishara's home for refreshments and a midday meal. The afternoons and evenings were spent visiting neighbors, competing in endless games of backgammon and cards, or just talking and gossiping. The Sunday after Black Saturday was no exception.

Everybody woke up early on that day. Mr. Bishara didn't wait for the rest of the family to get ready, and as usual, he went to church by himself to attend the mass from its very beginning. The Coptic mass lasted for a few hours, and only the most devout of the parishioners attended the mass for its entirety. The majority, however, went at different times depending on their piety and tolerance, as the ritual demanded from the congregation to stand most of its duration and recite the prescribed prayers in the Coptic language, which they didn't understand anyway.

By the age of seventeen, David had already read the whole Bible. Very rarely did he miss going to church, Sunday school, confession, or communion. At the same time, he had a good knowledge of the Muslim faith, as his education at school included the study of the Koran. His attachment to Eva made him especially aware of the conflict between the different religions, and he was always questioning the validity of them all. Although he was still a believer at heart, his intellectual curiosity and self-interest drove him to explore every antireligious philosophy that came his way. On that particular Sunday, it wasn't doubt that prevented him from going to church; it was a pressing urge to visit the previous day's scenes of destruction.

When he reached the tram stop, he was surprised to see Magda standing on the station's platform. The whole display that he had witnessed the day before at the Faculty of Fine Arts, where she was holding the hand of another man, came back to haunt him. He wondered if she was going out to meet that man. She couldn't possibly be going to the university, as all schools and universities were closed after the burning of Cairo.

"You're not going to the university today, are you?" he asked, after a quick greeting.

"Actually, I am," Magda said.

"But the university is closed today. Do you have a date with the man I saw you with yesterday?"

"Beautiful," she exclaimed in apparent anger, "so you're spying on me. David, I do like you, but I have my own life to live. It is very hard to explain everything now. I'll do that some other time. So wait until then. Don't do something foolish that might ruin my reputation."

By then, the next tram arrived. When he tried to follow her, she faced him with determination and said, "Don't come with me. I have a special meeting that has nothing to do with you."

He thought of following her, but he stopped as her words echoed in his mind. *She was a fully grown-up woman and had her own life to live,* he admitted. *She was entitled to do whatever she wanted. Wasn't he also in love with another person?* The thought of Eva lessened his misery and brought him back to his senses. He took the next tram on his way to the midtown area.

Walking through the streets of his beloved Cairo and seeing the destruction everywhere, he recalled the refrain of his primary-school history teacher, "It's up to your generation to rid our country of the foreign occupier."

Maybe his generation had started its mission, he thought, *but at what price?* The fires had consumed most of the historical landmarks of midtown Cairo. Whether these landmarks were owned by foreigners or not, they were still Egyptian landmarks. They were part of the history of Egypt, and history should be preserved, not destroyed. Is it the fate of Egypt that destruction would follow each successive foreign newcomer? He assured himself that Egypt had survived all invaders since the end of the Pharaonic Period. What had become of the Greeks, the Persians, the Romans, the Arabs, the Turks, and the French? He asked himself. They had all gone. And the British too would ultimately go as well. He found it a grievous misfortune that forced the poor Egyptians to pay a high price from their own wealth to foreigners, who systemically exploited and ransacked his country's treasures. Egypt would, nonetheless, survive. He had no doubt about that.

The midtown area looked like a ghost city. Very few adventurous people were in the streets. Policemen were guarding some of the foreign buildings that escaped the destruction, and cleaning crews were clearing the rubble. He stood in front of the Shepheard Hotel, wondering what would become of this symbol of foreign influence and domination. The remaining parts of its damaged façade stood ragged in the air, and its gaping holes revealed a blackened and desolate interior. He figured out that the building would be condemned. Yet he felt a great relief for the expected end of that symbol of a detested era in his country's history.

He walked through the fashionable Fouad Street until he reached Cinema Rivoli. He was glad to see that the fire didn't destroy it completely. This was the cinema that he loved the most for its architectural beauty and especially for its unique program, which included a live organ recital before the featured film. "I hope that the organ had survived." He verbalized his thoughts in a muted voice.

He glanced at the towering building of the Supreme Court, which stood in the center of the square across from Cinema Rivoli. He was always in awe of that building for the spaciousness of its marble steps and the height of its imposing columns. He gave a sigh of relief, as he discovered that it had escaped the destruction. But he would have felt otherwise if he knew its true nature, for in fact, that building was one of the glaring symbols of foreign domination of Egypt. Foreign aliens were immune from the reach of the Egyptian law; they were treated favorably under a more lenient jurisdiction in this fortress of the privileged Europeans.

He retraced his steps and turned right on Suleiman Street. The music of Sousa echoed in his head as he passed across from Cinema Metro, where they regularly played Sousa's famous marches after the end of each show. The building was blackened by smoke, but the damage appeared to be minor. *Sousa's music would still be played in it soon,* he figured.

He passed by more burned buildings, mostly cabarets, bars, and restaurants. In Kasr El Nile Street, the cinema that carried the same name escaped the burning, apparently due to its recessed location at the end of its own passageway. The Library of Arts was immediately next to that cinema, and that's where he ended his tour.

The Library of Arts was a novel place in the middle of Cairo, known only to a select few who were especially interested in classical music and art. It used to be a small historical villa before it was donated by Hoda Sha'rawi, the leader of the modern Egyptian Feminist Movement, to house art books and a huge collection of classical music records. The living room was comfortably furnished for the convenience of the listeners, who, not withstanding the interior coziness, invariably preferred to stretch on the grass of the library's garden amid an array of sculptures by famous Egyptian artists to listen to their favorite music through loudspeakers scattered at strategic corners.

David walked through the garden and entered the villa. He put his request for Verdi's *Requiem,* found the libretto with the English translation opposite the original Latin words, and sat in the garden ready to digest the whole experience. If history of Egypt had inspired Verdi to write *Aida,* he decided that there was nothing more fitting to lament the destruction of Cairo than listening to the requiem of the same composer. He fell in a trance the moment he heard the opening murmur of the muted cellos, which ushered in the chorus singing "Dona eis, Domine" followed by "Kyrie eleison." When the "Dies irae" first section began, he followed the English translation, and as he read the words "*Heaven and earth in ashes ending, day of wrath and doom impending,*" he couldn't help but wonder how the requiem expressed what he had already seen in the burning of Cairo. He closed his eyes and concentrated on the music when the "Confutatis" and "Lacrymosa" sections began. He didn't open his eyes until the chorus and the soprano joined each other to repeat "Libera me" twice to end the requiem.

Verdi's music was still echoing in his head when he returned home. The house was filled with every immediate and distant relative. To his relief, nobody had noticed his absence. He stealthily joined in the festivities as if nothing had happened, but his mind was busy, thinking of Eva, Magda, religion, and the charred buildings of Cairo.

The following few months passed peacefully with nothing dramatic to distract him from his studies. One more year and he would enter the university. *So would Eva,* he reassured himself. To his surprise, he didn't feel too bad for the apparent end of his relationship with Magda; an ever-present sense of betrayal had always tarnished that relationship. With Magda out of his life, he felt worthy of Eva's love. Their separation would finally come to an end, and he was confident that their love would endure. And he believed that, somehow, they would fulfill their childhood dream and get married. But the unforeseen events of the rest of 1952 and the subsequent developments changed everything.

THE REVOLUTION

The yearly summer exodus from Cairo usually began immediately after the end of the school year. The well-to-do families ran away from the oppressive heat of Cairo and headed to Alexandria. The less fortunate ones searched for inexpensive resorts, somewhere along the Mediterranean, and the poor just stayed in Cairo. Out of the large numbers of vacationers who went to Alexandria, only a minority kept apartments there year round. The rest rented a place for the summer, for one month, or just for a few days, depending on their means. The Bishara family was one of the lucky owners who kept an apartment in Alexandria.

Alexandria, the second largest city in Egypt, was originally a small Pharaonic town, which was absorbed in the bigger metropolis that Alexander the Great had built on the Mediterranean coast. Subsequently, and in succession, it became the capital of the Hellenistic, the Roman, and the Byzantine Egypt for almost a thousand years, until the Islamic conquest of Egypt.

Modern Alexandria boasts of one of the most famous and fashionable seaside boulevards, the Corniche, that stretches along the Mediterranean shore from Kotb Bay Citadel in the west to the king's palace, al-Montazah, in the east. A few jetties, man-made or natural elevations from the rocky bottom, extended into the sea and separated stretches of named beaches along the coast. Restaurants, casinos, and private clubs were built on some of these jetties. However, no residential buildings were allowed on the seaside of the Corniche except in Stanley Bay area, where a c-shaped hill enclosed an exclusive beach. A row of cabanas stretched at the bottom of that hill, and two tall apartment buildings towered on its western end. The Bishara family's apartment was in one of those Stanley Bay buildings.

David accompanied his family to their summer residence in the summer of 1952. Once everyone had settled down, his father and his brother Joseph shuttled back and forth between the two cities, according to the demands of their work. In their absence, David, as the only male present, assumed the responsibility of caring for the females who were left in his custody.

Every day he carried chaise-longs, unfolded them under the beach umbrella, and stretched there with his sister and sister-in-law, reading one of his books. Or he joined them for a swim or a game of racket ball, while his mother stayed in the apartment to prepare their midday meal. They all returned to the apartment at noon for lunch and siesta. In the evening, they took their showers, splashed their faces with their favorite cologne, dressed in fashionable clothes, and descended for a stroll on the Corniche. They invariably headed east to Sidi Bishr, the hub of the summer vacationers, where everybody intermingled with everybody else, ate roasted corn on the cob, licked ice cream cones, enjoyed succulent cactus fruit, or just conversed with friends and acquaintances they happened to meet.

The rocky bottom of Sidi Bishr Beach jutted from the water in different areas to give it its characteristic appearance. Across from a cove of calm waters, the rocks formed an island that became the destination of expert swimmers. The Royal Automobile Club, on the rocky eastern corner of the same beach, was an impressive and exclusive building reserved for the wealthy and frequented by the king and his circle of close friends. Regular people were not privy to what went on inside it. However, rumors of immoral acts, sexual escapades, and degenerate behavior of the king and the club members added more fuel to the popular resentment against the aristocratic and the privileged class of the country. Still, people looked at that club with awe and envy.

David also went to Sidi Bishr when he happened to have a free day for himself. On that trendy beach he would meet with some of his school friends, walk on the Corniche, or swim the hundred yards or so to the rocky island to bask in the sun with other boys and girls, away from the watchful eyes of their elders.

When his father or Joseph were present, everybody would be treated to a tram ride to the midtown district to see an American movie in one of the modern cinemas or have dinner in the famous Greek Casino in Al Shatby Beach, where a live show with music and dancing accompanied the traditional seafood meal. Occasionally, David joined his brother for a male-only evening at the Teero, a shooting club west of Shatby Beach, where they would spend a few pounds betting on skeet shooting, where professional target shooters aimed at discs launched into the air over the Mediterranean waters.

The summer days proceeded in this fashion until July 23, 1952.

On Wednesday, July 23, David woke up early as the sunlight started to illuminate his room. When he opened the radio, the call to the morning prayer, Al Azzan, made him realize that it was still too early to stir or make any noise that might disturb his sleeping family. He lowered the volume and continued to listen as his mind wandered, as usual, into the mysteries of the three monotheistic religions. When he looked to the east, he saw the orange-colored disc of the sun rising above the distant horizon and gradually spreading its light over the sleeping city, as scattered noises from the traffic and voices of people increased to announce the beginning of a new day. *No wonder,* he thought, *that his ancestors worshiped the sun.* A new revelation suddenly flashed through his mind—*what does it matter if we called this life-giving power sun or God?* He concluded that religion was not the final truth but an attempt to explain the unknown, a necessary effort to make sense out of the limited knowledge available to humans. *If religion were man-made, as it appeared to be,* he reasoned, *it shouldn't stand between him and Eva.*

An unexpected announcement from the radio interrupted his musings. It was exactly six o'clock in the morning when he heard the voice of an officer with the name of Anwar Al Sadat reading a proclamation from the Revolutionary

Council of the Free Officers announcing the start of the Egyptian Revolution of 1952 from the studios of the State Broadcasting in the name of Mohammad Naguib, the new Commander of the Armed Forces.

The rest of the family woke up when David raised the volume to make sure of what he was hearing.

"What's going on?" David's mother asked, as she entered the living room.

"It is the revolution," he told her as she listened to the rest of the announcement. "It'd happened," he said.

"It's about time," she said. "But I am afraid that a civil war will ensue. There might be a lot of killing, which makes me worry about your father in Cairo. I hope that he is safe."

Both of them rushed to the balcony, overlooking the Corniche, when they heard the newspaper boy yell with excitement, as he stood at the corner selling his newspapers.

"Read about the revolution," the newspaper peddler chanted as he stretched his hand with copies of "Al Ahram" and "Akhbar Al Youm," the two major daily papers. "Long live the new revolution!" he screamed as his customers snatched copies from his hand.

"Go down and buy the newspapers," David's mother said.

When David came back with the newspapers in his hand, he kept one for himself and handed the other to his mother. Front-page headlines announced the revolution in bold print. It was true; thirteen members of a revolutionary council had executed a peaceful and a bloodless revolution in Cairo. They reassured the population that the revolution was enacted in their name and for their benefit and to give the country back to its legitimate owners, the oppressed and forgotten working class.

The following few days ushered in fast moving events that culminated in the abdication of King Farouk on July 26. It was announced that the Revolutionary Council had given an ultimatum to the king through the newly appointed Prime Minister Ali Maher. "In view of your misrule, your violation of the constitution and your contempt of the will of the nation," the ultimatum announced, "the army, which represents the strength of the people, has ordered Your Majesty to abdicate in favor of the heir to the throne, Prince Ahmed Fouad, on this day, July 26, and that you must leave the country on the same day before six o'clock."

That turn of events didn't surprise anyone; the corruption, the womanizing, and the reckless behavior of that fat king were of legendary proportions. It was also a known fact that he himself didn't believe that he would remain on the throne for long. He actually was quoted as saying, "There would ultimately be only five kings left in the world, the king of England, and the four kings of the deck of cards."

The uneventful fulfillment of that ultimatum and the pageantry of the final departure of King Farouk took the country by surprise. At around six o'clock in the evening, King Farouk, in the uniform of an admiral and accompanied by his wife Narriman, who carried the new infant king in her arms, left Ras Al Tin Palace. As the Royal Yacht, the Mahrousa, left the harbor, a twenty-one-gun salute reverberated over Alexandria. No fighting happened, and no blood was shed.

David, like the rest of the Egyptian people, didn't personally see the departure of the king from his palace—there was no TV at that time—but he was standing on the Corniche among a multitude of onlookers as the Mahrousa sailed out of the country. He remembered his primary school teacher when he told the students about the other Mahrousa that carried Khedive Ismail during the ceremonies that accompanied the opening of the Suez Canal and wondered if this Mahrousa was the same one used by Ismail. No matter, the end of King Farouk's reign was the culmination of every Egyptian's goal, and David felt happy for that peaceful eventuality. He recalled the slogans he used to shout with the other students during their frequent demonstrations against the king, especially the one that said: "Ela Ankara Ya Ibn El Mara" (To Ankara, you son of the 'bad' woman). At last, he thought, he was witnessing the end of that foreign dynasty that ruled Egypt from the time of Mohammad Ali until that day. He only regretted that the revolution didn't abolish the monarchy for good, instead of keeping the line of ascendancy in the figure of the infant king. "Well," he echoed the declaration of the Revolutionary Council, "... at last, Egypt is going to be ruled by Egyptians for the first time since the time of the pharaohs."

The literal meaning of that declaration, though, had to wait for another year, during which the old system was gradually transformed into the new one. The titles of Pasha and Bay were abolished. Ali Maher was dismissed, and Mohammad Naguib assumed the position of prime minister. The royal properties were confiscated, and no one was allowed to own more than two hundred acres of agricultural land. The political parties were dissolved, and, finally, the monarchy was completely abolished and replaced by a republic with Naguib as its president. Soon thereafter, Naguib was deposed, and Gamal Abdel Nasser, the real planner and leader of the revolution, became the president and the ruler of Egypt. The transformation was thus completed.

The transformation of David was also completed at the same time. His break with Magda became final, and his attachment to Eva was solidified. Only one more year was left for him to finish high school and for Eva to join him at the university. His new concept of the word *God* and his new understanding of religion convinced him of the logic of detaching himself from his conservative society. It also convinced him of the real potential for the ultimate success of his original plan to run away with Eva and live permanently with her in a more tolerant country. The new revolution promised freedom and self-determination, and he became determined to assert his freedom and choice.

Back in Cairo by the end of the summer, he concentrated on his studies to attain the high grades necessary to enter medical school, in his quest to become a doctor in order to execute his master plan. Nothing distracted him from pursuing his goal. There was no more need for political activism, as the revolution had accomplished all of what the dissidents wanted. The country was rid of the monarchy, the aristocracy, the feudalism, and the political parties, and it was on its way to end the foreign occupation.

He graduated with honor, submitted his application to the medical school, and eagerly waited for an opportunity to go to Kantara.

THE VESPA

"You did your part," Mr. Bishara told David as they took the tram to the Vespa dealership in Ibrahim Pasha Street, "and I'll do mine." He then continued in a proud voice, "You didn't only graduate with high grades to qualify you for medical school, but you also came on top of your class. You will get the Vespa, as I have promised you."

A quick lesson from the dealer was all that was necessary for David to learn how to drive his new Vespa. Once the deal was finalized, he drove his father to his work, went to the Motor Vehicle Department, registered his new vehicle, and passed the driver's test before going home to his waiting mother.

"You really deserve it," his mother said, as she descended to the street to look at the Vespa. "It is beautiful. It took a lot of convincing to let your father agree to buy it for you. Now that you have it, you don't have to struggle with public transportation to commute to the university. Not too many kids your age have the luxury of owning their own vehicle."

"I know," he said. "I really appreciate all what you have done for me. Five years ago, you gave me a violin. Now father has bought me a Vespa. I am thankful for all of that. I have to think of a car when I graduate from medical school."

"Don't be greedy," his mother said. "When you graduate from medical school, you should be able to make your own money and buy your own car."

Back in the apartment, his mother mentioned that she was planning to go to Kantara, where Victoria was getting ready to deliver another child.

"I won't be going to Alexandria this summer," she told him. "However, you can go with your brother and his wife."

This was the opening that he was looking for. He must go to Kantara and see Eva.

"I would rather go to Kantara with you," he said. "Who knows, may be this is my last chance to visit the place of my childhood and see my old friends there."

"I don't have any objection to that," she said. "Maybe you can take me on your Vespa."

"Would you let me do that?" he asked with apparent excitement.

"Of course not," she said. "I was just kidding. I'll take the train, and you can come with your Vespa, if your father agrees."

"I'll depend on you," he said, "to get his approval. Would you do that for me?"

"I'll try," she said.

She did, and his father agreed.

"You can take your friend Hassan behind you on the Vespa. I'll take your suitcase and violin with me. See you in Kantara," his mother said before she boarded the train.

Hassan was staying with them, as he too was applying to the medical school. Both friends were ready to go to Kantara by the time David's mother had left. A few days after her departure, David got on the Vespa with Hassan and drove the scenic route to the Suez Canal.

Ismailia was their first stop, and they couldn't resist exploring that historic city on the banks of Lake Timsah, as they remembered the lessons of their primary-school history teacher.

The city that Ismail had founded impressed them more than they had imagined. It was an ultra-modern city with a grid of straight streets. Most of its houses were whitewashed Mediterranean villas with red-tiled roofs and lush, well-kept gardens. Sandy beaches on the lake were within a walking distance from the city center. Ismailia housed the headquarters of the Suez Canal Company, and it was the bedroom district for the mostly foreign employees of that company and for the officers of the British occupying forces. (The Fayed Military Base, near Ismailia, was still in the hands of the British army.) The sporting clubs were reserved for the foreign expatriates, and local Egyptians were not allowed to join them. Everything in and around the city made the two friends feel strangers in their own country.

After a sightseeing tour in the city and its neighborhoods, they took the road that ran parallel to the canal on their way to Kantara. The canal itself was hidden from their view as it traversed its course below the level of the desert's floor. You couldn't have guessed its presence except when convoys of ships sailed by. Even then, the ships appeared to be floating in a hidden trough, with only the upper parts of their hulls showing in a surreal scene, as if from a fairy-tale performance. Nowhere else in the world could you witness such a view.

The two friends stopped a few kilometers north of Ismailia and climbed the sandy hills to get a better look at the ships that happened to be passing in the canal. David stood there, waving at the sailors who stood on the decks of those ships. He recalled his ever-present determination of immigrating to America. *He was on his way to becoming a doctor, and someday, after he would have graduated from medical school,* he thought, *he would seek a job on one of those ships and end in America where he would live happily with his Eva.*

"Tell me," he addressed his friend, as a frightening thought crossed his mind, "do you remember Eva, the girl who attended the primary school with us?"

"Of course I remember her," his friend answered him. "How could I forget her when she is the prettiest girl in town? I know that a lot of men tried to marry her, but it seems that she rejected all who have approached her parents with a marriage proposal, preferring to get a university degree first."

Those words fell as music to his ears. *The gods must have been on his side,* he thought. He didn't care if the gods were Jewish, Christian, or Muslim, as long as his plans were proceeding in the right direction.

The smell of the freshly cut alfalfa on the left side of the road mingled with the crisp air of the desert on its right side, invigorating the two friends as they resumed the drive north until they reached Al Kantara Gharb and boarded the ferry on their way to their final destination.

The gods must have surely been on his side, David thought, as he saw Eva and her parents when he entered his sister's house.

"Do you remember Uncle Mohammad and his family?" his mother asked him, after the initial greetings.

"Of course, mother," he answered with a quivering voice as a fluttering feeling in his chest overwhelmed him. Thankfully, Uncle Mohammad's voice calmed him down.

"What a handsome young man you have become," he heard him say. "I remember you as a child when you traveled with me in the caboose on that fateful journey out of Palestine."

"I'll never forget that trip," David said, "nor would I forget what followed." He looked at Eva from the corner of his eye. She got his message, he was sure; her lips stretched in a captivating smile.

"I heard that you are going to medical school," it was Eva's mother who spoke those words.

"Yes I am," he said. "How about Eva?" He continued as he found a chance to get the information he wanted.

"I want to go to medical school as well," Eva said. "But…"

Her father interrupted her. "Nonsense," he said. "A girl like you should think of marriage and not be wasting your time in unnecessary education. Remember that I had respected your wishes when you objected to all the men who wanted to marry you. I'll let you go to the university but not for seven years. Medical school is too long for a girl. You'll be an old maid by the time you graduate and finish the necessary training. Four years in the Faculty of Liberal Arts is all that I will agree to. You can become a teacher, have enough time to get married, and raise a family. That's final."

"That's fine with me, Dad," she said, "as long as you don't force me to get married."

Her mother interfered. "Would you two stop this argument in front of other people?" She said in an angry voice. "We have settled this issue a long time ago. Let's talk about something else."

"How about the revolution?" Mr. Mohammad said.

"Not again," his wife interjected before he had a chance to expand on his patriotic sentiments. "You know that I am as Egyptian as all of you, but I don't trust this Nasser. He seems to be heading to a holy war against everything foreign or Jewish. Let's hope that he doesn't ruin the country by another destructive war."

David's mother, sensing the gathering of a stormy cloud, wisely changed the subject by turning to her son.

"David, I have brought your violin with me. Why don't you play something for us? How about Abdel Wahaab's overture, 'The Nights of the Arts?'"

David obediently brought his violin, tuned it, and started to play. The first three notes formed a harmonic cord and lead to a melancholic melody. A series of stepped-up scales of five notes each followed until two repetitive beats brought the theme to its comfortable end. He repeated the same melody in a higher octave then brought the whole piece to its dramatic conclusion. He transferred his emotions to the music as if to send a message to the one who was the recipient of his love. Her facial expression showed that she did receive his message, but in that setting, she was incapable of voicing her own response. Her mother was the first one to speak and thus relieved her of that duty.

"David," Eva's mother said, "that was wonderful."

"I knew that something good would come out of you," Mr. Mohammad said, "but I didn't imagine that you'd be that good." He then looked at Mrs. Bishara and said: "I guess he is taking after you in his musical talent."

The music did lighten their moods, and they conversed in more entertaining subjects until the end of the visit.

The next evening David went to the cemetery. Eva was waiting for him in their familiar place.

"I knew I'd find you here," he said as he embraced her.

"I," she said, "knew too that you would come here."

Eva disengaged from his embrace as if shocked by an electric current.

"I am afraid I wouldn't be able to stop if we kept holding to each other," she instinctive expressed her fears. "We're not children any more. God knows how far we would go to if we don't stop now."

"I know," he said. "I love you too much to cause you any harm."

"I managed to stay wholesome and pure," she said, "and I'll stay that way for you."

A deep sense of guilt overwhelmed him as he listened to her words and recalled his sexual encounters with Magda. He wanted to confess his infidelity, but he decided otherwise, as he convinced himself that his relationship with Magda didn't diminish his loyalty to Eva and that the adventure had ended anyway. He finally said, "I'll remain as wholesome and pure for you too." He then recalled the discussion she had with her father the day before. "Yesterday," he said, "I realized the hardship you went through with your parents, which makes me more determined to succeed and be more deserving of your love. But tell me, how did you manage to convert your father?"

"As you know by now," she said, "I refused all the marriage proposals that came my way. In the end, my parents had no choice but to let me go to the university. True, I wanted to go to medical school, but if the price I have to pay for my freedom is to go to the Faculty of Liberal Arts instead, so be it. This would buy us more time, until we could immigrate to America as we have always planned."

A gentle desert breeze rustled the leaves in the treetops. The ensuing sounds delivered the two lovers into a transcendental realm, as if they were elevated to a higher level of consciousness where all the sensory perceptions disappeared. They didn't know for how long they stayed in that trance until Eva broke their enchanted silence.

"Wouldn't it be nice," she asked, "if you could play your violin here?"

"Oh," he said, "how I would love to play for you alone! Unfortunately, I can't do that, or else the whole town would find our hideaway."

"But yesterday," she said, "I felt that you were playing for me only."

"I was," he said. "Actually, I was playing for you during the last few years. Somehow, I believed that the air would carry the vibrations of my music on its waves and travel the distance to you. Even if you didn't hear it as music, I was sure that some energy would reach you—some mysterious energy more powerful than words or touch or music."

"You certainly have a marvelous way of expressing yourself, whether in music or in words," she said. "You make me feel too insignificant next to you."

"Nonsense," he said.

"No," she said. "It is not nonsense. I really mean it. Here you are playing the violin and talking about waves and energy and things I don't understand."

"You will, Eva," he said. "You will, if you read the books I have read. In fact, what I know, I know because of you. You remember the first time we talked together when we were in primary school? Both of us were perplexed about religion, the war, and our future. Since then, I took it upon myself to find a way to overcome all the obstacles in front of us. I studied the three religions and read about philosophy and other branches of human knowledge. It's a big world out there."

"You frighten me, David," she said. "You have grown up so much that I can't catch up with you."

"You will," he said. "You will, Eva. I'll teach you. I'll share my knowledge with you. I'll read books and recite poetry for you. I'll play and listen to music with you. We'll grow up together. Don't forget that I have the advantage of studying science on my way to medical school. That has opened a new world for me. It is unfortunate that they separate the students in high school for the study of liberal arts for some and the study of science for others. You wouldn't know how wonderful it is to study biology, chemistry, physics, and mathematics. All these disciplines opened my eyes and made me look at religion with a different light. Now I can see very clearly that religion will not be an obstacle between us—not if we leave this country."

"I wish I had your confidence," she said. "However, I'll take you on your word. By the end of this summer, I'll be in Cairo. If you promise to teach me what you know about science, I promise to teach you what I know about liberal arts."

"It's a deal," he said.

He grasped her hand and tried to pull her close to him but she resisted.

"Now," she said with determination, "you want to break our promise to each other. We just have to keep our purity for the time being. Besides, it's getting late and I have to go home right away."

"Am I going to see you again?" he asked her.

"I'll try," she said as she walked away.

That night, David couldn't fall asleep. He recalled all their conversation word by word until the moment he held her hand. As he closed his eyes, the memory of her touch spread a dizzying feeling all over his body. When he was about to fall asleep, he felt as though Eva had dissolved in his blood and become a permanent part of him. Unable to have her in person, he was content to have her in fantasy, and it was inescapable that he continued to have her in his dreams. When he woke up next morning, the fire was still burning in his veins, and Eva was still under his skin. He walked aimlessly until he found himself standing at their favorite spot in the cemetery. Nothing would have expressed his feelings except poetry, and a new poem started to germinate in his head. He quickly returned home and drafted his verse. It took him the rest of the day to revise his composition until he wrote the final draft.

That same evening he waited for her in the cemetery. She came. He didn't try to touch her or even open his mouth. He just gave her the piece of paper with his new poem. She couldn't read it in the dark, so he recited the poem for her.

Come share with me,

The life I have, the life to be.

Come share with me,

Sunshine, rebirth, and ecstasy.

The songs I played and sang again.

The poems I read and scanned again.

The dreams I thought and dreamed again.

Come share with me,

This harmony,

From which I weaved,

A melody,

A glorious symphony,

Waiting for you.

Tears started to flow down her cheeks, and this time around, she couldn't resist. She embraced him and showered his face with kisses until she found her way to his mouth. He tasted her salty tears and felt her pliable body, and the whole world disappeared from his consciousness. He felt nothing but the presence of Eva in his arms. She reciprocated his embrace and became oblivious to her previous promise. She couldn't stop embracing and kissing him until they had satisfied their pent-up desires without the need for actual intercourse. It took Eva a few minutes to gather her composure.

"I love you, David. But we have to stop before we do anything rash," she finally said. Suddenly, and without giving him a chance to say anything, she untangled herself from his embrace and ran away to her house.

He didn't see her again until the night before his departure when her family came to say good-bye.

"Soon enough Eva will join you in Cairo," Mr. Mohammad said at the end of the visit.

"Where is she going to stay?" David asked.

"At my brother's house in Giza," her mother answered. "Actually, my brother lives very close to the university, and Eva can walk to her school from there."

David's mother kissed Eva's cheek as she was leaving. David was content to grasp her hand and press it tenderly, as if to transmit all what he couldn't verbalize in front of everybody. She reciprocated his pressure as their eyes met. Silently, they communicated with each other without the need for words. There was no doubt in their minds about their commitment to each other and the ultimate success of their plans. And the first step in their plan was about to begin. Eva would go to the university, and she was on her way to Cairo by the beginning of the next school year.

CAIRO UNIVERSITY

On the first day of the first year of medical school, David drove his Vespa out of Shoubra until he reached Ismailia Square. He was tempted to go southward to Kasr Al Eini Street, where his medical school was, but he knew well that he had to spend the first year in the Faculty of Science, in the main university campus at Giza. He thus headed westwards and crossed Kasr Al Nil Bridge to Gezira Island. Another bridge took him to Mourad Street, and from there he was on his way to the university.

He drove through the gate and turned around the rotunda. The Faculty of Liberal Arts was the first building to his right, and he stopped in front of that building for a moment. *"Here we are, Eva. I'll keep my promise,"* he whispered as he continued his drive to the Faculty of Science, located at the back end of the campus.

Hassan was waiting for him. After the customary Middle-Eastern embrace, they walked toward the lecture hall for their first class.

"Have you seen Eva?" Hassan asked as they took their seats.

David wasn't prepared for a question like that. After some embarrassing silence, he responded with his own question, "Why do you ask?"

"Oh, come on, David," Hassan said. "I know that you have a crush on her, and I saw you stop by her school."

He wasn't sure how much his friend knew. If Hassan had known something, could it be possible that other people might have also discovered his secret? He had to be cautious.

"Suppose I do," he said, "why that would be of your concern?"

"Nothing," his friend said, "I am just worried about you. This is a Muslim country, and a Muslim girl wouldn't be allowed to marry a Christian boy."

"But she is half Jewish," he said reflexively.

"According to the Muslim religion, she has to follow her father, who is a Muslim. If he finds out that you are going out with his daughter, he will surely get her out of the university and force her to marry a Muslim man. Someone might see you with her and tell her father. I am just warning you to be careful. There are plenty of Christian girls in the university, and I am sure that you can date any one of them."

How could his friend have known? Could he tell on him? He wondered. It was prudent to play it safe.

"There is nothing between Eva and me," he finally said.

The noisy chatter around them suddenly subsided, and they also had to end their conversation, as a teacher entered the lecture hall.

"I am going to teach you Latin," the teacher began. "Most of the medical terms you'll come across are derived from Latin or Greek. It will be easier for you to understand medical terminology if you find their Latin or Greek roots."

What a wonderful way to start a university education! David thought.

Lectures on biology, botany, chemistry and physics followed and David eagerly absorbed all the knowledge that came his way. The atomic theory, the periodic table, and the Newtonian laws of motion intrigued him. Gradually, a universal order became apparent, but this wasn't enough for him to reach a conclusion about religion, predestination, and free will in his ultimate quest to save his relationship with Eva. He had to wait until he saw Einstein's equation, $E=MC^2$, when he realized a basic continuum in nature that allowed him to formulate a personal opinion about everything in life, as he understood it at the time.

What to do about Eva was a different story? His friend's warning troubled him and kept him from looking for her. That is until he couldn't wait any longer. He saw her for the first time at her school when he was assured that Hassan wasn't around.

"We shouldn't meet where people can see us," he said as he led her to an isolated corner.

"What's the matter?" She asked.

"You remember Hassan, my friend from the primary school?"

"I do. He attended the same Kantara High School with me."

"I think he is spying on us."

"What makes you think that he might do such a thing?"

"I had a long conversation with him. He mentioned our different religions and hinted that someone might tell your father about us. He actually said that if your father found out about us, he would certainly take you out of the university and force you to marry a Muslim man."

"You frighten me by this talk."

"It frightens me too. We just have to be careful. A lot of students know our families. We shouldn't meet each other here. I thought we should meet in isolated places like the Orman Garden or better still the Fish Garden in Zamalek. We both don't have classes on Thursday afternoons. How about meeting me at the Fish Garden next Thursday?"

"It seems that you have thought of everything. The Fish Garden is fine with me."

"I have to go now before somebody sees us. I'll see you next Thursday at noon."

"See you next Thursday."

They met in the Fish Garden every Thursday. Some Thursdays, they stayed there, holding hands when nobody was in sight or just talked about their newly acquired knowledge. On other Thursdays, he took her on the Vespa to the pyramids, the desert of Heliopolis or the Kanater Al Khaireya. In each outing, they discussed literature and science, or read books together. Their sensual impulses subsided gradually as an intellectual friendship dominated their encounters. They became contented to hold hands or exchange an innocent kiss when circumstances permitted.

"I finished reading the *Merchant of Venice* last week," he told her in one of those outings, sitting under the shadow of the Great Pyramid.

"We are still studying this play at school," she said, "but I have finished reading it too. What do you make out of it?"

"I love its poetic language, especially in Act V, Scene 1, where Lorenzo opens the scene with the refrain: 'In such a night…when the sweet wind did gently kiss the trees, and they did make no noise.' Eva, I am no Shakespeare, but I remember such a night in the cemetery when I wrote a poem for you."

She was listening to him with rapture as if in a trance. *Yes, she remembered that night,* she told herself. She even memorized the poem he had recited in the dark. She cried then, but now her emotions were more of awe and adoration than emotional. No tears wetted her eyes.

"On that night, however," David continued, "When you had left me, the desert wind did make a noise. When the sweet wind kissed the trees in the cemetery, they actually made the sweetest music I'd ever heard. You can understand how I feel when I listen to Lorenzo talking about music when he says, 'The man that hath no music in himself, Nor is not moved with concord of sweet sounds, Is fit for treasons, stratagems, and spoils. Let no such man be trusted. Mark the music.' I wish I have my violin with me to let you listen to the sweet sound of music."

Eva couldn't hold her tears any longer. It took her a while to regain her composure and respond to his eloquence.

"How I wish I can memorize verse and express myself in words as you do," she finally said. However, unable to say anything else and reluctant to express her emotions by a physical contact in a public place, she found it more fitting to return to the *Merchant* and her studies.

"But," she said, "you allowed your romanticism to distract you from the main plot of the play; the revengeful justice of Shylock."

"Fine, let's talk about that. I see Shylock acting like every other Jew; his main interest is profit and money."

"You too are stereotyping the Jews as greedy and vengeful," she said as she walked away from him in anger. When he caught up with her she turned around and faced him with a determined expression. "Can't you see," she said. "That's what is troubling me. Don't forget that I am half Jewish. I do have a problem with how Shakespeare depicts the Jews and how you willingly agree with him."

"I don't mean to offend you," he said as he tenderly held her hand. "Personally, I have nothing against the Jews. However, I do have some reservations about religions per se whether Jewish, Islamic, or Christian. If you actually look deeper into the character of Shylock, you'll find that his behavior has nothing to do with religion but everything with how badly Antonio had been treating him. When it comes to explaining the true humanity that he shares with the rest of the Venetians, Shylock says, '…Hath not a Jew eyes, hands, organs, dimensions, senses, affections, passions, as a Christian?' Then he is most convincing when he says, 'If you prick us, do we not bleed?' That's how we should look at everybody, in a human context and not in a religious one. If it might comfort you more, I have found out that Antonio's justice is not much different than that of Shylock. After his eventual triumph, Antonio disowned Shylock of his treasure, his daughter, and even his religion. Let me tell you, Shylock's forced conversion to Christianity would not have changed his heart. I bet he must have remained a Jew inside."

"I didn't see it this way," Eva said as his words had gradually dissipated her anger. "May be I am more sensitive than you are in virtue of my maternal inheritance. How about this Jacob and the Laban story? Where did it come from?"

"Oh, that one about the ewes and lambs and streaking. It is from the Bible."

"There is no Bible in our house."

"You should get one now that you are beyond the watchful eyes of your father. Just ask your Jewish uncle to give you one."

"Are you trying to convert me to your religion?"

"On the contrary, I see all religions as equally coming from a questionable source. Some other time, I'll have to explain to you what I mean by that. I have my own theories."

"What are they?"

"You have to read the Bible and the Koran first. Then you have to understand basic science, which is the ultimate and only truth."

"I will, if that's what it takes to understand you. I'll get a Bible, and I'll read it. However, basic science is beyond my reach. Why don't you explain it to me?"

It was in the desert of Heliopolis when they returned to that subject again. A small park at the edge of town, facing the eastern desert, reminded them of the British cemetery in Kantara—the same eucalyptus trees, the same sandy walkways, but without the crosses or the tomb markers. Beyond that park, there were no buildings. Two roads diverged at that area, one to Cairo international airport and the other to the city of Suez. Only a handful of cars used those roads. In fact, private cars were a rarity in the streets of Cairo in the early fifties. Without too much traffic around it and with rarely a pedestrian in sight, that park gave them a perfect place for solitude and privacy.

Eva had only read through the first half of Genesis, but she had already made an educated opinion.

"What a weird book it is," she said after they had settled under the shadow of a large tree that gave them added protection from any possible watching eyes. "God appears to be brutally vengeful, illogically biased, and indecisively hesitant."

"The God of the Koran is even more brutal and biased. Now you understand what I mean."

"There is no hope for us if we follow the teaching of these books."

"There is hope, if we see beyond these books."

"What do you mean?"

"Now you should be ready to grasp what I mean."

From a kiosk at the entrance of the road to Suez, a smell of grilled shish kebab wafted through the air and excited their appetites. Leaving Eva in the place, David drove his Vespa to that stand and bought two sandwiches. Back in their hidden spot, they resumed their discussion as they were finishing their meal.

"Let me start with some scientific theories," David started. "All matter is constructed from the same building blocks: electrons, protons, and neutrons. Their numbers in each atom determine the different composition of every known element in nature. And every particle is energized by its own specific electric charge in a continuous motion or vibration the speed of which is dependant on the atomic number. The lower the atomic number, the faster is its vibration until you reach the highest vibratory speed, the speed of light, where matter itself is transformed into energy. Einstein discovered the formula that joined matter and energy in a simple equation: $E=MC^2$."

"Slow down," Eva interrupted him. "It's very hard for me to picture these particles and atoms."

David smoothed a stretch of sand between them and drew with his finger a sketch of an atom, with a nucleus dotted with neutrons and protons and circled with smaller dots representing the electrons. He explained what was meant by positive and negative charges and their affinity to attract or repel each other.

By then, the afternoon hours were winding down. It was time for them to go home. When they reached the Vespa, David brought out a physics notebook from its side compartment, gave it to Eva, and asked her to read it until their next meeting on the following Thursday.

After a week, they headed to the same park in Heliopolis. Eva had already read his science notebook and was ready to make the leap from the physical facts to the philosophical abstractions he was about to explore with her.

"Fact, matter cannot be created or destroyed," David said when they had settled down under their favorite tree. "This makes me question the concept of mind, or soul or spirit or whatever we mean by these names—what are they, where do they come from, and to where they are heading? I personally believe that our minds are but an expression of energy, the result of a transformation of matter in our brains through chemical reactions into energy."

He looked at Eva to make sure she was following that line of thought. She wasn't about to distract him with any further questions, so she said nothing.

"The higher the vibratory energy reached in any particular mind," he continued, "the higher that mind stands in the evolutionary scale. Knowledge, understanding, music, love, and such elevated human experiences propel a person, a mind, to a higher level of vibration, or energy, until it reaches the highest energy possible, or what religions call God. But, this God, if there is a God, is much better than the God of the religious books. He must be the all-inclusive law that is encompassing all the known scientific and moral laws. He cannot be revengeful or biased, and he cannot change his mind or else everything will collapse. This is the perfection—the encompassing mind that all humanity is instinctively striving to attain during its long evolutionary history. From this perspective, I see death not an end in itself, but rather a transformation from a matter state to an energy state of being as part of a universal and cosmic unity. The level of vibration attained before death is the level that we keep in the afterlife, the level that adds toward the perfection of the universal whole. The higher it is, the closer we are to perfection, i.e. God. This might explain the religious understanding of heaven. As for hell, there is enough of it here that there is no need to extend its scope beyond this life. I think that religion got it wrong in this respect."

"You confuse me. First you are against religion, but then you are trying to reconcile the religious teachings with your scientific theories. You have to choose between the two."

"You misunderstand me. True, I am against religion, but I see its teachings as the accumulated wisdom of the ancients. This wisdom was built on the limited knowledge of their time, and I am sure that it was thought of by individuals of higher vibratory energy in an attempt to explain the unknown. Science is discovering new explanations that should correct the misunderstanding of previous human ignorance."

"I don't think it is that simple," she said. "There must be an innate something in the human being, something that drives us to yearn for eternity, something that's spiritual with a soul, and something with attributes of its own beyond matter and energy."

"If it is true," he said, "that this soul, this something, is beyond matter and energy, there is no hint of its existence. No such soul ever came back to reveal its presence. No human senses or scientific tools have ever detected it. And how come that we still describe it with terms that apply only to matter and energy? How come we talk about heaven and hell, reward and punishment in physical terms where the 'physical' is not supposed to exist in the afterlife? There would be no nervous system to feel the pains of hell or the joys of heaven."

"I can't explain that," she said. "I guess we are limited by our human dimension to be able to describe what is beyond its limits."

"Again," he said, "you're insisting on the existence of something beyond our limited dimensions and the known laws of nature, which is a logic I am unable to comprehend. I am just saying that religions pretend to know what this some-thing is, while science stops at what we know for sure and doesn't speculate on what is beyond the known facts."

"We are going in circles," she said. "The two of us can't resolve this issue at the present time. Let's continue this debate some other time."

"I agree," he said. "But that other time might be numbered in a couple of weeks, as you'll be going to Kantara for the summer vacation."

"I know," she said. "I can't imagine that our first year in the university will come to an end in two weeks. You and I should concentrate on preparing for the final exams of the year, which means that we shouldn't see each other until after that."

Nothing more was said, as they walked toward the Vespa. When they reached a safe distance from Eva's house, they parted at an isolated corner.

"Until then, Eva," he said.

"Until then, David," she responded as she walked away.

They met only one more time after the school year had ended. He drove her to Al Kanater Al Khaireya, where they spent a whole day together.

What a difference six years could make, David thought as he recalled his first visit to the Kanater. An older girl had awakened his sexuality at that time and had satisfied his physical needs for a few years. He didn't feel any regrets from that relationship. On the contrary, he thought of it as a necessary right of passage that rid him of the perplexity of the teenage years and carried him safely to a comfortable balance. *Sex without love is just that, sex,* he thought, *but love transcends the physical needs.* That's why he never slept with Eva, he reasoned, but he ignored the fact that all his meetings with Eva during the previous year had occurred in public places where physical intimacy was impossible.

They were walking on the body of the dam holding hands when he asked her, "Are you going to wait for the result of the exam before you return to Kantara?"

"No," she answered. "My father is coming tomorrow to take me back. My uncle will send me the result."

"Does this mean that I am not going to see you all summer?"

"I am afraid that this is true," she answered.

If this was to be their last meeting, David thought of doing something memorable to fall back on until the next school year. He thus took her for a rowboat ride on the river. Far away from the shore and beyond the reach of watching eyes, he let the boat drift and sat down next to her. The warmth of her body transmitted a delicious sensation through him, and he couldn't resist anymore. His arms enclosed her, and his lips found their way to hers. They remained so absorbed in that position that they didn't realize that their boat had drifted toward the shore. Only when they heard someone shouting at them that they returned to the real world. By then, a few people had already gathered on shore, screaming and laughing at them. When someone tried to turn over the boat, its owner intervened and allowed them to step ashore.

"You have desecrated my boat," the boat's owner screamed at them. "Don't you ever come here again. This time, I'll let you go, but if you linger around any longer, I'll call the morality police."

As they ran to where the Vespa was parked, a volley of stones came their way, but fortunately none hit them as they managed to distance themselves from their pursuers and drive safely out of the park.

"I am sorry, Eva," he said as soon as they were at a safe distance.

"Don't be silly," she said. "This is not your fault. I am equally to blame as you."

"Still," he said, "I should have known better not to kiss you in a public place."

"I shouldn't have reciprocated your kiss," she said. "That makes both of us equal in guilt."

"If this were guilt," he said, "I would love to be guilty all the days of my life."

"Not in such a scene," she said. "You can imagine what they would have done if they knew that we belonged to two different religions."

"They are just an ignorant mob," he said. "What matters is that we love each other, which is beyond their comprehension. We know that this society wouldn't allow us to be together. We'll find a way to defeat this society and enforce our will."

"I hope so," she said, as she re-enforced her response by holding tightly to him as the Vespa sped away.

GRAVEDIGGERS

O n the first day of the new school year, David drove to Kasr Al Eini, the Medical School of Cairo University, which was a large complex centered around three university hospitals.

The "new" university hospital was a row of medical specialty wards and operating rooms aligned on the eastern bank of the Nile. Several laboratories and X-ray facilities, in addition to the Faculty of Dentistry and the Faculty of Pharmacy, were housed in separate buildings. A sports complex, including a field for football, tennis courts, and an outdoor café, spread across from the hospital. A dormitory for the nurses and another separate one for the interns and residents completed that campus. A high fence surrounded the whole complex.

The "old" university hospital was separated from the new one by a canal that joined the Nile a short distance to the north, across from the affluent district of Garden City. Ancillary buildings included several amphitheaters, anatomy, physiology, and chemistry laboratories, and two museums—one for anatomy and another for gynecology. These two museums boasted of extensive medical specimens, universally renowned for the excellence of their educational content. A cafeteria, a music room, a lounge, and a recreation room added extra space for relaxation and creative activities for the students. A short bridge, over the canal, connected these two hospitals.

The third hospital, the Children's Hospital, was located a short distance from the old one, in the impoverished district of Abu Al Reish.

The palace of Prince Mohammad Ali was the only other building in that part of Manial, the island that was enclosed by the Nile and the Kasr Al Eini Canal. The northern tip of Manial remained as a preserved peninsula until recently, when a luxury hotel, the Marriott, was built on it.

David acquainted himself with and used all the facilities of the medical school, but the anatomy laboratory became his favorite hangout. The first time he entered the place and smelled the formaldehyde fumes emanating from the corpses that stretched on rectangular metal tables, he felt a special, enduring attachment to the human body. Even when several of his colleagues fainted and some threw up, he internalized the whole scene with excitement. It was early on in that lab that he became adept at using the surgical instruments and performing the required dissection proficiently. And, he decided to become a surgeon.

As he acquired more knowledge about the human body, its anatomy, physiology, and chemistry, he became better acquainted with life itself. Science, he was sure, would ultimately solve his personal problem. In a few years, he would become a doctor, he would then seek employment in one of those ships his teacher was talking about, take Eva with him, and settle in America where they would marry and live happily ever after.

Away from the university campus in Giza and very much involved in his studies, David found it difficult to see Eva as frequently as he did the year before, especially because her uncle had inexplicably restricted her freedom. On the rare occasions that they managed to meet, they hardly had enough time to continue their customary discussions in science and English literature, but they were content with those stolen moments and happy to be close to each other.

When summer vacation arrived, David went to Kantara with the excuse of driving Hassan home. A surprise was waiting for him—Mr. Mohammad had divorced his wife. A rumor was circulating in town that Mrs. Mohammad couldn't tolerate her husband's jealousy and his violent temper anymore. She had taken her daughter and fled to Cairo. Mr. Mohammad, with no power to fight his wife's influential and wealthy Jewish relatives, had no choice but to divorce her and accept his daughter's decision to stay with her mother's side of the family.

The news devastated David, and he didn't know what to do. He considered seeking Eva in Cairo, but he suspected that her Jewish family would prevent her from seeing an Egyptian boy. *To wait for the beginning of the new school year, when he would easily find her, away from the watching eyes of her mother and relatives would be the better choice,* he thought. He decided to stay in Kantara for a few more weeks.

One day, as he was reviewing Gray's Anatomy with Hassan, he wished he had a human skeleton in front of him to orient himself with the anatomical descriptions he was supposed to visualize.

"It would be much easier to study if we had an actual skeleton," he said.

"I know where to get one," Hassan said. "I have a friend who took me to the Indian cemetery, out in the desert. You can go with him and dig a skeleton for yourself."

"How about you?" David asked.

"Grave digging is not for me," Hassan said. "My religion forbids me from doing it."

"How about the anatomical dissections you have been doing for the last year? Isn't that against your religion too?" David questioned him.

"That's different," Hassan said. "Somebody else is responsible for getting the corpse, not me."

"I think that is hypocrisy," David said. "By your dissection, you are in fact violating the sanctity of the dead."

"I know that," Hassan said, "but it is justified for the sake of learning."

"Then for the sake of learning, you should come with me and get your own skeleton. In fact, religion shouldn't worry you. I am more worried about finding a putrefied corpse underground. It would be frightening to dig out a shriveled and smelly one."

"Not really," Hassan said. "My friend discovered the place when he found human bones exposed in the desert. I inspected the bones with him, and they were perfectly clean. The flesh must have disintegrated in the dry desert heat."

"You'll come with me then?" David asked him.

"I'll go if nobody else knows about our adventure." Hassan said.

"How about your friend?" David asked. "Don't we need him to show us the place?"

"No," Hassan answered him. "I know the place myself. We can go there early in the morning before the sun gets high in the sky and heats up the desert.

Before sunrise on the following day, the two friends, armed with two shovels and plastic bags, walked the few miles to the site of the Indian cemetery.

"How do you know that this is the place?" David questioned his friend when he stopped at a nondescript stretch of desert.

"You see that pile of stones?" Hassan said. "That's how my friend marked the site where he had found the bones. I helped him to bury them back in the ground."

They stood there not knowing where to start the digging.

"OK," David suggested. "Just tell me how the bones were aligned, and I'll tell you where to dig."

"They were aligned the same way as the long axis of this pile of stones."

"We have to assume," David explained, "that they had buried the dead parallel to each other. If we dig on either side of your stones, we are bound to find other skeletons. You start at the right, and I'll start at the left. Let's go."

It wasn't too difficult to remove the first layers of the loose desert sand. After that, they came across more compact layers, and they had to be more careful. Soon enough, Hassan's shovel hit something hard.

"Come here, David," he yelled at his friend. "I must have reached the burial area. Let's dig together here."

They unearthed a long bone, clean as ivory without any attached muscles or ligaments.

"You see my point now?" Hassan said as he held the bone. "It is clean as a whistle."

David took the bone to inspect it.

"It is the right humerus," he said.

"Yes, it is," his friend agreed. "This means that the rest of the skeleton should be to the left side of this bone. We have to dig in that direction."

They continued to remove the compact sand slowly and deliberately. When a whole skeleton was exposed, they stood gazing at it and at each other.

"This skeleton is yours," Hassan said after a moment of silence. "Collect all the bones in your bag and make sure to get all the small bones of the wrists and ankles. In the meantime, I'll start digging at the other side for my skeleton."

At the end, each one had collected the bones of a complete skeleton.

"You see, Hassan," David said as they started on their journey back to town, "there was nothing to it. Do you feel that you have committed any sin or crime?"

"No," Hassan said. "Actually, I feel a sense of accomplishment, and that worries me. I know that what we have just done is against my religion."

"You will get over this feeling," David said, "as you got over your fainting spells at the beginning of our dissection course."

The two friends never discussed the subject again, as the grave digging gradually disappeared from their conscious memories.

Back in Cairo, David tried to find Eva in that large city without success. He kept on going to the neighborhood of her uncle's house, hoping that she might show up, but she didn't. Finally, he learned from one of her neighbors that her family had gone to Marsa Matrooh, another Mediterranean resort, for the summer. He decided to wait for the new school year when he would see Eva at the university. In the meantime, joining his family in Alexandria seemed to be a good distraction.

Befuddled by the unknown fate of Eva, he couldn't enjoy the usual summer activities. The beach, the sea, and the Corniche ceased to excite him. Nothing succeeded in blocking Eva from his mind except his books and his violin. It wasn't until July 26, 1956, the fourth anniversary of the ousting of King Farouk, that other events drew him out of his self-imposed isolation.

On July 23, the anniversary of the revolution, the celebration in Cairo included the usual speeches and fanfare. However, the military parade of that year was different. Egypt had bought modern arms from the Soviet block in a daring challenge to the western powers that had denied them to Nasser, when they were generously giving them to Israel. The newly acquired Soviet arms were openly displayed in that celebratory parade in obvious pride and determined challenge to the western powers. Still, all that wasn't unusual during the geopolitical reality of the Cold War Era. Moreover, the western powers didn't even have any hint that the president of Egypt had another soon-to-be revealed weapon in his arsenal that threatened to heat the cold war into a hot one.

On July 26, 1956, David was standing among the huge crowd that converged into Manshiat El Backry Square in Alexandria, in anticipation of the next move from Nasser. Everybody was fixing his gaze on the balcony of the Bourse, where Nasser was to appear to address the crowd and, as it turned out, the whole world. It was the same balcony that had witnessed the attempted assassination on his life two years earlier. David recalled what happened since then.

Instead of succeeding in killing Nasser, that failed conspiracy, in fact, elevated him from a behind-the-scenes mastermind of a revolution to the undisputed leader of the whole country. He deposed Mohammad Naguib and appointed himself as president and supreme ruler of Egypt. His progressive social and patriotic agenda elevated him into a messianic figure in his country and the Arabic world. He then aligned himself with Nehru of India, Teto of Yugoslavia, and Suharto of Indonesia to propel himself onto the world stage, at a time when the precarious balance between the two superpowers was threatening world peace, if not a devastating nuclear annihilation. A new, nonaligned movement, or Third World Power, was born, and Nasser used this new power to his advantage.

At seven o'clock on July 26, Nasser appeared in the balcony of the Bourse. His towering figure and stern face galvanized the crowd into a frenzy of cheering, despite the looming and threatening clouds over the fate of Egypt. Nobody guessed what was in store for the world when he started his speech by recounting the history of the building of the Suez Canal in the relaxed, colloquial Egyptian Arabic. David knew exactly what Nasser meant when he mentioned the name of Ferdinand de Lesseps and his exploitation of the Egyptian Khedive, as he recalled the lessons of some earlier years, including the one in front of the statue of that same de Lesseps in Port Said. However, he became uncomfortable when his hero started to make fun of Mr. Dulles, the American foreign secretary, and Mr. Black of the World Bank, for reneging on their promise to finance and help in the building of a new high dam in the south of Egypt at Aswan that would preserve the wasted waters of the yearly flood and make use of it to reclaim agricultural land from the desert and generate much needed electricity. Then suddenly, a bombshell exploded.

"Egyptians!" Nasser said in a determined, angry voice. "For too long we have been robbed by that imperialist company, that state within a state, the International Naval Company of the Suez Canal. But we shall be robbed no more, for I can tell you now that at this very moment, the canal is being nationalized, and its premises taken over. From tonight, the Suez Canal belongs to us. Do you hear me?"

Nasser broke into a fit of laughter when he saw the expected reaction from the crowds. "The canal will pay for the dam," he continued after the cheering had subsided. "The canal was built by Egyptians. It was built on the skulls of our countrymen. 120,000 Egyptians died digging it. The United States and Britain were going to offer us seventy million dollars to build the dam, but the income from the canal is one hundred million dollars a year. In five years, that means half a billion dollars. Let the Americans choke on their fury. We do not need them. The dam will be built by Egyptians. To hell with America! Do you hear me?"

Nothing in the history of the world compares to a challenge from a small country to the most dominant power of the time. Others might have seen that action as a reckless maneuver by an inexperienced leader, but not the Egyptians. The mass of cheering and dancing multitudes that flooded the streets all over Egypt must have sensed that that moment was the most dramatic in their country's history. At last, they could lift up their heads, as their leader never tired of repeating, and become the masters of their own destiny. At last they were on their own, without any foreign power to exploit them, tell them what to do, or rob them of their country's wealth.

David joined the celebration with the enthusiasm of a believer, as he recalled his primary school teacher and his calls for struggle against all foreign domination of Egypt. His previous doubts about his leader's challenge to a superpower evaporated as he, like everybody else, was overtaken by the assured temperament of Nasser. *If Nasser dared to do such a thing,* David thought, *he must have known what he was up to.* The consequences were immaterial. Somehow he had confidence that Nasser would carry the country safely through any future difficulty.

As the world was heading into a momentous crisis, the ordinary Egyptians continued in their daily routine. David, too, was distant from the evolving world affairs, as he resumed his second year at the medical school. One issue remained to be settled—what happened to Eva? With no presumption to secrecy, he dared to go to her school and waited for her in the cafeteria.

"What happened?" He asked, as he led her to a remote corner.

"I am not sure," she said. "You remember long time ago when I told you that there was something mysteriously wrong with my parents?"

"I remember that very well," he said. "I thought that they had some conflict because of their different religions."

"Maybe," she said. "When my mother took me with her to Cairo, we stayed with her Jewish family, who helped her to get the final divorce. With more help from her influential Rabbi, she managed to get legal custody of me. She even changed my name to her Jewish maiden name. She had said that according to the Jewish law, children of Jewish mothers should be raised Jewish. I am officially Jewish now."

David didn't know what to make out of that dizzying transformation. He reflected for a moment on all possible outcomes.

"Eva," he finally said, "something good might come out of this divorce. First, your religious identity is finally defined for you. Second, if you're Jewish, it would be much easier for us to get married than if you are Muslim. There's still hope for us after all."

"I thought of that, too," she said. "Maybe that's why I am not too much depressed by this divorce. The only thing that bothers me is that my mother might force me to marry a Jewish man. 'You shouldn't repeat my own mistake and marry an Egyptian. You should marry a Jew,' she keeps telling me."

"At least, a Christian would be more acceptable than a Muslim."

"I don't know, but I see your point. I'll have to work on that. We'll figure out something before we graduate from the university."

"The future for us doesn't look that bad after all."

Reassured by that conclusion, they looked at each other with adoring expressions. No physical contact was possible in a public place, but eye contact was a satisfying alternative.

"Are we going to see each other again?" David asked when the time came for them to part.

"I don't know," Eva said. "My mother has become worse than my Jewish uncle in restricting my freedom. She has been acting strangely lately. I heard her telling her family that she doesn't want to deal with Egyptians anymore. She said that the Egyptian government is conducting a virulent anti-Jewish propaganda, which is not only threatening the safety of Israel, but also that of the Jewish Egyptians. She is already talking about leaving Egypt and going to the United States. She made me promise not to get involved with any Egyptian. I am afraid that she might take me away from you. But strangely enough, I don't feel bad about that—I mean leaving Egypt. If that happened and I ended in America, you could join me there. Our plan might come to fruition after all."

"It is a storm that will ultimately pass," he said. "Let's wait and see what the future brings."

"We have no choice but to wait," she said.

They didn't have to wait for long as the events of 1956 unfolded precipitously.

The nationalization of the Suez Canal Company was a tremendous blow to Great Britain and France, who were the majority stockholders. They secretly made a deal with Israel to invade Egypt, which would give them a pretext to occupy the Canal Zone and put an end to the rule of the belligerent Nasser.

On Monday, October 29, 1956, Israel attacked Egypt. Britain and France, in a surprising and unreasonable ultimatum, demanded an immediate cease-fire and the withdrawal of both the Egyptian and Israeli armies to ten miles from the canal, or else they "would intervene in whatever strength may be necessary to guarantee freedom of transit through the canal," despite the fact that the Israeli army was nowhere near the Suez Canal. In fact it was actually nowhere within two hundred kilometers from there.

The timing and language of that infamous ultimatum exposed the Tripartite Conspiracy, and alerted the Egyptians to take a drastic action. When the British and the French started bombarding Port Said, Nasser immediately withdrew the Egyptian army out of Sinai to save as much as he could from the newly acquired Soviet arms and to concentrate on defending the mainland of Egypt.

By the time the allied armies of France and England landed in Port Said, the world opinion was completely on the side of Egypt. A UN resolution was passed demanding an immediate stoppage of the hostilities. But what ultimately saved Egypt was the stark reality of the Cold War—Russia threatened to bomb London and Paris, and America took a resolute stand against the British and the French. That disastrous episode in world history ended by the withdrawal of the French, the British, and the Israeli forces from Egypt, but the world would never be the same.

The triumphant Nasser unleashed a vengeful campaign against everything foreign and anybody of Jewish descent. After breaking the diplomatic relationship with Britain and France, he seized theirs and the Jewish properties. He then ordered the expulsion of all the fifty thousand Jews in the country, although most of them had lived all their lives in Egypt, and none of them knew of any other place that they could call home.

Eva and her mother were among the multitudes of Jews who were forced to leave Egypt. Like the rest of the departing Jews, they remained under strict surveillance by the secret police until their departure, and David didn't have a chance to see them or say good-bye. His first option was to get out of Egypt right then; but his attempt at getting an exit visa failed. The Egyptian government had put restrictions on travel, and an exit visa was required to even get a passport. His devastation was so severe that he began to question the authority of the revolution. He might have fallen victim to depression, or he might have put himself in danger's way by working against the revolution, except that his determination to become a doctor ultimately saved him. *Only then,* he thought, *would he be able to control his destiny and free himself from the restrictive culture he abhorred.* As for Eva, he figured out that she was safe from the religious conflicts of the Middle East. She must have gone to America, where most of the deported Egyptian Jews went. If that turned out to be the case, then half of their plan would have been accomplished, as she had previously told him. He would eventually find a way to join her.

As the universities were closed during the course of the crisis, David used that forced vacation to study his textbooks. At the same time, he practiced on his violin and continued reading English literature, as he had done when Eva was around. By the time the doors to the university opened again, he was already ahead of his class. The rest of the year was uneventful, and he easily passed the year-end exam.

Gradually, his sympathies with the Egyptian revolution started to diminish as he saw the confederation with Syria come and go and the name of his country changed to the "United Arab Republic." To him, the name "Egypt" represented a continuous history of more than 5,000 years. All that history was abolished by a name change. Similarly, foreign languages were banned, and to his dismay, the importation of foreign textbooks was prohibited. The only personal benefit he gained was his disengagement from his usual involvement in the political organizations. If he had to become a prisoner in his own country, he should better concentrate on *his medical, literary and musical studies until he graduated from medical school,* he concluded.

When he finally graduated with distinction, his joy wasn't complete. The only person with whom he wanted to share that moment wasn't there. Worse, he still had no clue to her whereabouts. He never received any letters from her. There were no more Jews in Egypt who might have any knowledge of the fate of her family. Even if he managed to get out of Egypt, despite the failure of his renewed attempts, the chances of finding Eva seemed to be very remote, if not impossible. He concluded that staying in Egypt, at least for the time being, was inevitable. He had no choice but to make the best out of his circumstances. But his certainty of seeing Eva again never ceased.

His love of surgery made him seek a residency in that field. His grades qualified him for a residency program in the university hospitals, and for the following two years, he lived there almost all the time. Nothing distracted him from his training and studies not even the war that Nasser had started in Yemen.

After he had finished his training but failed, again, to get a passport and an exit visa, he opened an office in the district of Ghamra, next to the Coptic hospital, where he served as a surgeon on its staff. His dedication to his work took him away from everything else until Magda reappeared in his life.

GARCONERA

After Eva's departure and during the remaining five years of the seven-year medical school, David remained faithful to Eva; he never forgot their vows to stay wholesome for each other. He resisted the temptation to seek women, similar to the majority of his colleagues, which wasn't too difficult to do, considering the still-vivid memories of Eva and the intensity of his studies. It wasn't until his internship and residency, when the separation from Eva became long standing and leaving the country appeared to be impossible, that he couldn't resist any longer. Ultimately, he had to satisfy his sexual needs like everybody else. How could he have resisted any longer when his work had brought him in close contact with nurses and inevitable temptation?

It was customary for two or more young men to rent an apartment, or Garconera, where they could indulge their sexual needs in secret. When Hassan approached him, David agreed to share a Garconera with him. Whenever he had a date with an available nurse, he just made sure that his friend wasn't using the apartment and headed to the safety of that hiding place. Once he started, he couldn't overcome the addiction, as if in revenge for the drought he endured for the previous long years, especially now that a choicest supply of hospital nurses offered him endless recruits. Most of the available women were virgins, and it was customary not to violate their virginity. Rubbing from outside, or what was traditionally called "brushing," was the accepted practice in these circumstances. A non-virgin nurse was a rare and welcome find. David had to accept, like everybody else, whatever came his way—outside brushing or the real thing.

One night when he was in bed with one particular virgin, whose looks reminded him of Magda, the act of brushing brought back his pubertal experiences so vividly that he imagined that Magda was the one lying under him. From that moment, he couldn't resist an urge to find her. A quick inquiry revealed that Magda had been married to a relative of hers, and that she had become very active in the artistic community, which propelled her to the higher ranks of Cairo socialites. To his surprise, and as if fate was working behind the scene, he found out that she was about to open a special exhibit of her paintings at a famous gallery in Zamalek, the wealthy district in the center of Cairo.

He went to Zamalek for the opening night. The gallery occupied a stepped-down apartment in an old building on a side street. He descended a few steps down from the street level to find himself in what appeared to be a foyer that opened into several side rooms. In one of those rooms, a crowd of men and women, with drinks in their hands, was gathered around Magda, the apparent star of the evening. He immediately recognized her despite the long intervening years. But he had to admit that the young girl he remembered from his days in Shoubra had become a mature woman, bursting with sensuality and assertiveness. She appeared to be flirting with all the men in the room. He recognized some of the faces in the crowd—the minister of culture, one or two of the leftist writers, some shabby-looking men and women whom he assumed to be fellow artists, the man he had seen with Magda on that fateful day at the Faculty of Fine Arts, and a few blonde women who were certainly of foreign origin.

"David," Magda screamed as she broke away from the crowd and rushed to greet him. With nontraditional public daring, she planted a kiss on his cheek as she affectionately embraced him. Still holding his hand, she introduced him as Dr. David, her neighbor from Shoubra and an artist in his own right, though not on canvas but on the violin.

"Don't run after the Russian girls, they are already taken," she whispered in his ear when she noticed the direction of his gaze. "I hope that you're here to see my paintings and not to flirt with me like the rest of these men."

Was that remark an invitation or a warning? *At least,* he thought, *it was promising; he just had to wait and see.* He stayed close by her side to find out, but she was busy talking and laughing and kissing every man in sight. Her openness and daring shocked him, but deep inside, he comforted himself that such a free-spirited woman would be more receptive to his advances. He could wait for another time to try his luck with her. For now, he was content to look around and familiarize himself with her work and friends. Appetizing hors d'oeuvres were spread on a side table, next to a wide variety of soft drinks, wine, vodka, and scotch. He wondered if he was still in Egypt, the conservative Muslim country, or if he was witnessing a mirage. He pinched himself to make sure of what he was seeing. Finally, he had no choice but to join in the feast. He sampled the food and ended up with a glass of wine in his hand. One of the female artists approached him.

"So, what type of doctor are you?" She asked.

When he answered her question, she took him by his hand to a man whom she introduced as a doctor and a writer. David wanted to engage him in literary discussions, but the writer was interested only in women and sex. David had to excuse himself to get another drink. The female artist returned to introduce him to other guests, more writers, artists and a few of the employees of the ministry of culture, including the minister himself. One of the blonde girls was talking in a foreign language to a foreign man. The man introduced himself in broken English as the Russian cultural attaché in Cairo. The girl was one of his office staff and a close friend of the Egyptian minister of culture. The Russian attaché whispered in David's ear an Arabic word equivalent to "girlfriend," to clarify what he had meant by "friend."

When he had heard and talked enough, David withdrew to see the paintings. He was impressed by the balance of Magda's compositions, the boldness of her brush strokes, and the choice of her themes, which depicted scenes from the daily lives of folkloric Egyptian characters: the eternal fellah with his ancient tools, the southern cane-dancers with their elegant movements, the legendary "Bent El Balad" with her sensual body curves and inviting expression, and the desert nomads with their dancing Arabian horses. He detected a transparent harmony on each canvas, as if an inaudible music was emanating from the flat surfaces. He wasn't surprised that she managed all that harmony; after all, she was also a piano player. Audio and visual training were implicitly expressed in her paintings.

"What do you think of Magda's paintings?" The voice of Monir, one of the leftist writers, intruded on David's solitude. Not waiting for an answer, Monir continued, "Apparently, you don't remember me. I was one of the student movement's leaders with you. It seems that your medical studies had taken you away from the revolutionary movement. Do you still write poetry?"

A pictorial reel from his high school years unfolded in his mind. The face of Monir filling some of the frames stood out. It was the same face that he was looking at.

"Yes, I remember you. You are Monir from Tawfikia High School," David finally said. "And yes, I still write poetry, but in a different venue."

"I still remember some of your political verse. You certainly had a talent for words. The revolution is still going on. The socialist change we are witnessing is just a step in our struggle to spread the inevitable, worldwide communist order. If I remember correctly, you were a leftist revolutionary yourself. Most of our generation's revolutionaries have ascended to leading positions in the arts, the universities, the news media, and the government. It would be beneficial for you to join our group. We conduct regular meetings at the Russian Information Office, which gives us access to books, vodka, and Russian girls, if any of that is of interest to you. Here is my telephone number. Call me when you're ready."

David was in no mood to write for the revolution. He didn't mind, though, the vodka and the Russian girls. However, reluctant to voice his thoughts and hesitant to state his political opinions in public, he said: "I am too busy with my medical practice that I don't even have the time to scratch my head."

Thankfully, the reception was winding down, and the guests were starting to leave. One of the Russian girls took Monir's hand and led him out of the gallery. David left empty handed.

Wow, he thought as he walked in the streets of Zamalek. Here he was a doctor, with many years of education and training, hardly managing to make a living. The circle of people he worked with could never afford the extravagant life style he had witnessed at the gallery. Every day, he dealt with sick, poor, and needy patients who had no idea about fancy hors d'oeuvres, let alone hard liquor. Was he dreaming or did he actually have a glimpse at the privileged society of Cairo? What he had seen during that evening revealed the presence of new bourgeois elite confined within a circle of writers, artists, and government officials, who appeared to be isolated from the harsh reality of the ordinary Egyptians. He realized that his medical career had isolated him from the vibrant intellectual and privileged circles of Cairo of the early sixties. *If he was destined to stay in Egypt,* he thought, *he better join that elite group.* The promise of vodka and Russian girls enticed him. However, he decided to postpone getting in touch with Monir until he had tried his luck with Magda. He decided to go to the gallery the following evening.

Only a handful of people were present at the gallery that night. Magda was sitting on a chair in the foyer, obviously making herself available to the viewers of her art. She saw him the moment he stepped in.

"What a surprise," she said as she greeted him. "Two nights in a row? Is it the art or the artist you're interested in?"

"Both," he said as he understood the hidden meaning in her words.

"Let's start with the art," she said as she led him to one of the exhibition rooms.

David stopped at a particular painting that drew his attention the day before. It depicted a teenage boy in the foreground playing the Rababa, the one-string, primitive prototype of the modern violin. The boy's attention, though, was directed at a girl who had tilted her head in his direction, while she bent her body in a suggestive posture that showed her well-rounded buttocks through her transparent dress.

"Are you telling a personal experience here?" David asked.

"Every creative work must necessarily draw from personal experiences."

"That's what I have figured out. I am the Rababa player in this painting."

"Yes, you are. And I am the young girl who seduced you the first time."

"That's why I came back today. Yesterday, I wasn't sure. But now that I know I am still in your memories, I have to confess; this painting made me seek the artist."

She jerked her head in a sudden movement as if to thrust away a bundle of hair that was floating in front of her eyes. Actually, she was trying to hide the blush that had started to spread over her face. She was surprised at her reaction, but she immediately understood that the mature woman she had become had unconsciously regressed to the innocent days of her youth. And she liked that. She saw an adventure coming her way, but she instinctively chose to play the feminine role in a hunting game.

"But I am a married woman now," she said.

"Yes, I know. You had dismissed me before for another man. You can dismiss me again now, and I'll disappear from your life as you had disappeared from mine."

"But at that time, I didn't intend to make you disappear, and I don't want you to disappear now either. I tried to find you, but your sister Julia made me believe that you were busy. Were you in love with another woman?"

He didn't want to tell her about Eva, but seeing that Magda was ready to have him back, he found it necessary to tell her a convincing response without too much detail.

"Magda, I was in love with another girl. Circumstances prevented us from being together. That's all I can tell you."

"Poor David," she said. "I'll make it up for you."

"But you have just said that you're a married woman now."

"Yes, I am, but I am a free woman too."

"Your husband—is he the one I saw you with on that day at the Faculty of Fine Arts? I saw him here yesterday."

"No. I just keep him around if I happen to need him. My husband is in Yemen. I am married to an officer in the army, who has a tour of duty in Yemen at the present time."

David wasn't prepared for all that openness. "So you're one of those leftist radicals who were here yesterday," he said, in an attempt to hide his embarrassment.

"Oh, come on, David. Don't be judgmental. You know why you have come back to me. I have been thinking of you too. We are grownups now, so let's face the facts as they are. I am a free woman, and you can have me any time you want. I knew I wanted you the moment I saw you enter this gallery last night."

"Magda, I have no love left in me to give. Even if I told you that I love you, don't believe me."

"OK, I won't believe you. But still, say it and you can have me. I want you David."

"I want you too, Magda."

This time around, their intimacy didn't stop at the brushing level; both had become experienced adults. And they went at it all the way.

With the help of Magda, David became a member of the leftist group of Cairo intellectuals. He called Monir and joined his circle of writers and artists. He frequented the Russian club and the Russian bookshop in Zamalek and had a steady supply of vodka. But he stayed away from the Russian girls; Magda insisted on that. Gradually, his life fell into a comfortable routine, between his medical work, nightly partying with his new friends, and stolen moments of exhilarating encounters with Magda. However, all that glitter and sex failed to block Eva from his memory. He was willing to give up all that in a moment if there was even the remotest chance of finding Eva, and he still looked forward to the day he would be able to leave Egypt and start his search for the woman he loved more than anyone else in the world. However, the turbulent events of the Middle East took him to another direction.

THE YEMEN WAR

In 1960, the Egyptian government passed a decree requiring all graduate doctors, starting with the class of 1960, to serve in the public health-care system for two years. Interns and residents were granted automatic postponement, but following that, they were eligible for the mandatory service unless they had an approved job in the private or public sector. Fortunately for David, having a job at the Coptic Hospital had exempted him from that mandatory rural-health service. However, a different and hard-to-avoid service was looming in sight—he was eligible for the draft.

At that time, the Yemen War was in full swing, and the armed forces were in need of more recruits. While university graduates were drafted in the reserve and had to go through three months of training at the military academy at Fayed, a few in certain professions were just called whenever they were needed to serve in the army in their professional capacity. They didn't even need to go through any military training. David was one of the "lucky" professionals to be called for the latter service.

His first assignment was at Fayed, the strategic military base on the western side of the Suez Canal south of Ismailia, where the Egyptian army had replaced the British forces. David boarded a bus heading to the city of Suez and disembarked at Fayed junction, a few kilometers from the city. The bus stop at Fayed was a nondescript place in the middle of the desert, marked only by diverging dirt roads in all directions. Military vehicles passed him by, but none appeared to notice him. He was told that a car would be waiting for him at the bus stop to take him to the hospital, but no car showed up. After an hour of waiting, he gave up and hitched a ride to the Fayed Hospital.

The Egyptian army took possession of the Fayed Base after the British forces had vacated it following a pact with Nasser. It was a vast military complex that included warehouses for the military arsenal, an airbase, a military academy for the education of reserve officers, dormitories for the soldiers, and residential complexes for the officers and their families. The adjoining desert afforded the base with plenty of room for training practices and maneuvers, and the next-door city of Ismailia, with its exclusive sporting clubs and beaches at Lake Timsah, became the playground for the officers. Fayed hospital, like any other privileged military hospital, in contrast with the public and private ones, had state-of-the-art equipments and well-trained staff from all clinical specialties. David, as one of the few unmarried doctors, had a comfortable apartment attached to the hospital compound, and he stayed there for three months.

To his disappointment, his surgical skills were never challenged; no major injuries or surgeries came his way. To overcome his boredom, he volunteered to help his medical colleagues in the outpatient clinic. But that too didn't satisfy his professional needs; all he was treating were minor complaints like headaches, aches and pains, and diarrheas. His only consolation was a weekly three-day furlough to Cairo, where he indulged in the social circle of his newly acquired friends and enjoyed the company of Magda when she was available, or the Russian girls when she wasn't. All that changed when he was unexpectedly transferred to a fighting unit, destined to leave for Yemen.

As much as he resented his new assignment, which would necessarily take him away from the vibrant life of Cairo, let alone his ultimate goal of leaving Egypt, his voyage through the Red Sea ameliorated that resentment. He was assigned to travel in a cargo ship that carried the equipment of his unit. Only a handful of officers and doctors were on board, but none of who interested him.

For the most part, he stayed by himself with nothing much to do. In this forced seclusion, he had plenty of time to think about his relationship with Magda, the fate of his medical practice, his career, his prospects of leaving Egypt, and how in the world could he find Eva. When his ship finally docked at Al Hodeiyeda Harbor, the main port of Yemen at the Red Sea, he was still pondering these issues with no resolution in sight. Soon enough, a succession of events relegated his personal concerns to a remote recess in his subconsciousness.

The fighting unit, to which his mobile hospital was joined, was destined to camp along the mountainous road between Al Hodeiyeda and Sana, the capital city of Yemen, to safeguard that strategic part of the country. A day in the stifling heat and the suffocating humidity of Al Hodeiyeda drained all his energy. Everyone around him suffered as well from the onslaught of that intolerable weather that the prospect of military combat became a welcome alternative. Next day, orders to march to the battlefield couldn't have come soon enough.

The mountainous road between Al Hodeiyeda and Sana was the only paved road in the entire country. David rode in his jeep at the head of his medical unit, at the end of the convoy. The drive seemed to proceed smoothly during the first few kilometers, where the road stretched straight through the western plains, but everything changed once they started the steep, tortuous climb to the mountains. Cars, trucks, and tanks labored along the winding uphill curves, and some vehicles started to overheat and break down. His jeep seemed to be grinding up the road, as it passed one disabled vehicle after another. Soon enough, it too gave up and stopped completely, as hot steam spewed out of the engine. He stood aside, while the driver opened the hood to let the steam out and add more water into the radiator. The commander of the military unit was returning to check on the disabled vehicles when he spotted David standing alongside the steaming jeep. He recognized him as the new civilian doctor who had treated him for a minor ailment at the Fayed Hospital.

"Come ride with me, doctor," the commander said. "It is my turn to take care of you."

When David settled in the backseat, he didn't hesitate to express his thoughts.

"Why can't these vehicles navigate a road like this one?" he asked.

"You see," the commander started his explanation, "these are Russian cars and tanks that were designed for a colder climate. We have apparently over-worked them too much in our exercises and maneuvers back home, but that's what they are for. Don't worry. Our soldiers are well known for their hard work and ingenuity. They will manage."

David recalled a similar scene he had witnessed when he was a teenager back in Kantara during the days that preceded the 1948 War. But this time, he was sure, no fraudulent arm deals were to be blamed for the malfunction of these equipments.

"What will happen if the enemy ambushes us now?" He felt compelled to ask.

"This will not happen," the commander said. "This road has been secured by our forces long before…"

A hail of bullets interrupted his explanation. Everybody scrambled to hide from the incoming gunfire, but fortunately, the source of the firing was too far on top of the mountain to cause any damage or harm. A contingent of soldiers was immediately dispatched, and the rest of the men were ordered to return to their previous work as if nothing had happened.

"Is there going to be a big battle now?" David asked.

"No," the commander answered. "This seems to be the work of a sole Yemeni who, under the influence of Catt, was entertaining himself by firing at us."

"What is Catt?"

"This is a weedy narcotic plant. The Yemenis chew its leaves and get high from its juice."

When the convoy started to move again, David's jeep, similar to some other disabled vehicles, wasn't ready to move yet. He thus resumed the rest of the trip with his commander.

For the first time in his life, David witnessed the breathtaking scenery of the mountains that towered above patches of white clouds floating in the val-leys below. The mountainous terrain seemed more challenging than the peace-ful, open, green fields and sandy deserts of his country. David wondered if topography could influence the nature of a country's inhabitants. Whereas his own people, in a flat country, were peaceful and laid back, more thinkers and builders than fighters, could these mysterious and foreboding mountains make the Yemenis more aggressive and more adventurous? Or could it be that genes determined the difference?

"You see how these local people are gathering outside their villages to greet us?" The voice of the commander interrupted his thoughts. David wanted to contrast that with the firing incident they had witnessed, but he couldn't dare to challenge his commander.

"I know that the previous incident is disturbing you," the commander said as if he read David's mind. "This is my second tour in Yemen, and I know how the Yemenis behave and fight. Here comes the officer who went to capture the ones who shot at us."

"Sir," the officer said after he had saluted his commander. "There was only one Yemeni who fired at us as you had suspected. We brought him back without any fight, but he is so completely drugged from the Catt that we can't interrogate him now. I'll let you know what we'll get out of him when he sobers up."

"Thank you for a good job," the commander said. He then glanced reassuringly at David and resumed his conversation with the officer. "Can you report on the status of the rest of convoy?"

"The majority of the disabled vehicles are already fixed and have joined the rest of the convoy," the officer reassured him. "Your foresight, sir, in training our mechanics in fixing these Russian vehicles helped tremendously."

It was a bitterly cold night when they ultimately reached their final destination at the highest peak of the mountains. Being a non-career officer without any previous experience with different terrains or weather, other than the predictable ones of his own country, David wasn't prepared for that cold temperature. He didn't bring with him, neither was he supplied with, the necessary gear. When the rest of the career officers and doctors settled in their hastily erected tents and warmed themselves with their heavy covers, David unfolded a stretcher in his own tent and covered himself with a flimsy blanket he managed to secure from another doctor. It seemed to him that everyone was on his own to manage with whatever was available. That fact became more apparent when a battle erupted soon afterward.

When a convoy was ambushed on a side road, it became necessary to secure that road and punish the offending locals. The military commander wanted a doctor to accompany the fighting detachment, and the chief doctor of the medical unit assigned David to that job. Armed with meager supplies, David followed in his jeep.

It was a bumpy dirt road that they took, but for David, the thrill of adventure and the excitement of the unknown made the physical inconvenience more tolerable and even exhilarating. The overpowering presence of tanks, armored personnel carriers, and heavy-duty arms must have looked too intimidating for any Yemeni, who might be hiding in the mountains, to attempt an attack. Everybody proceeded with confidence, even when crackling of small firearms echoed from each side of the road. Suddenly, the tank at the head of the convoy stopped in its tracks. The whole column behind it became an easy target for the incoming bullets. Everyone scrambled to his fighting position, and an unbalanced battle ensued. A barrage of cannon shells and bombs streamed at the directions from which the bullets came, and a dozen or so soldiers were sent to capture the offending Yemenis. The battle ended victoriously in a very short time, though not before some Egyptian casualties were sustained.

David was crouching behind his jeep when an injured officer was brought to him, with frothy blood streaming from his mouth and with obvious stridor and noisy breathing. David immediately recognized upper-airway obstruction. A quick examination showed a bullet track through the neck. David knew that he had to perform a tracheotomy on the spot. With no hesitation, he injected a local anesthetic and made the skin incision. He quickly made an opening into the windpipe, but only then did he realize that he had no tracheotomy tube to insert into the open wound. With no hesitation, he cut a piece of the rubber tubing from his stethoscope, inserted it into the tracheal hole, and secured it in place with a bandage around the injured neck. He frantically propped up his patient in the jeep and speedily drove him back to the field hospital, where he cleaned the wounds, inserted a proper tracheotomy tube, and evacuated his patient to the central hospital in Sana. It took David a few days to recover from that incident. However, time failed to explain the apparently dysfunctional Egyptian army.

David lived in a tent for the next two years. With no further battles or injuries and no surgeries requiring his expertise, he did what every other military officer was doing in that war—he played endless games of backgammon, smoked free cigarettes, bought a lot of luxury items that were not available in Egypt because of the ban on all foreign imports, accumulated generous pay, and gossiped about the infightings that were going on among the increasingly bored army commanders in Yemen. However, he continued to do what other officers didn't do; he read extensively, listened to classical music on his transistor radio, and did some gardening in the area around his tent.

No more major battles occurred as the Egyptian army resorted to a different tactic in fighting the war in Yemen; they bought the loyalty of the tribal fighters with money. The officer who was assigned to deal with the local tribes became the most important person in the war effort. He was entrusted with large sums of cash to distribute as he deemed fit. Tribal chiefs from every neighboring village flocked to the Tribal Affairs Office, declaring their allegiance to the Egyptians and demanding handouts. The mission of the Egyptian army in Yemen had devolved into an endless and costly occupation.

David couldn't help but think of the aimless direction of a war that bankrupted the Egyptian treasury and corrupted the beneficiaries of that senseless occupation, whether they were the army's commanders or the profiteering Yemeni chiefs. Rumors of mismanagement and outright fraud circulated around with no one daring to check or investigate them. However, the most depressing situation was the sorry state of the conscripted soldiers whom nobody bothered to care for. When the officers were flown to Egypt for a two-week vacation after every two months, the soldiers stayed in Yemen for the duration of their tour of duty, which might last two, three, or even four years. The result was mental disorders and frequent suicidal attempts, driven by despair and depression.

One bizarre incident raised a lot of questions in David's mind. A conscripted soldier broke down under the accumulated stress. He started to speak in gibberish, which everybody claimed to be a foreign language—some of his fellow soldiers swore that he was speaking in Yugoslavian. David interviewed that soldier and diagnosed him with hysterical breakdown. The words uttered by that soldier weren't a language at all. *Even if they were,* he thought, *how could the other soldiers recognize it as Yugoslavian, when none of them had the faintest idea how that language actually sounded?*

Occasional missions to Cairo and his share of the two-monthly vacation kept David from losing his mind in the harsh environment of Yemen and the sorry state of what he was witnessing. During his time off, he used his ever-increasing savings to splurge in the decadent life of Cairo. The war gave him not only a sense of superiority, but it also made him aware of the vulnerability of the human life and his own mortality. His appetite for pleasure during those vacations was so voracious that he gorged himself with whatever his tortured-self fancied. Magda remained a willing companion, and with her, he ate in the most expensive restaurants, drank all the liquor he could tolerate, frequented the famous nightclubs, and indulged in endless sex. He even sought the company of the Russian girls whenever Magda was not available in his bed, risking her wrath if she had found out about his infidelity.

At the end of his two-years tour, he concluded that the Yemen War was a failure. In his judgment, it had only succeeded in corrupting the military leaders and denigrating the fighting capabilities of the Egyptian army. Any non-biased observer would have agreed with him that the Egyptian army had degenerated into an obsolete force incapable of fighting a modern war. All that was the more frightening as Nasser was apparently headed for a war with Israel. David had a premonition of an impending national disaster. However, he saw a more pressing and personal disaster in his own degenerate transformation that took him away from his life-long ideals and his commitment to Eva. He looked at his attempt to go to America as a duty he owed to Eva and himself. He was a completely changed person when he boarded the ship back to Egypt at the end of his two-year tour.

A career in Egypt ceased to be an option and leaving Egypt became his pressing obsession. In that state of mind, he found himself inside the US

Embassy where he submitted an application for an immigration visa, which, if granted, might help him in getting an exit visa and a passport. In the meantime, he managed to get a discharge from the army. Waiting for a response from the American Embassy, he had no choice but to make a living by reopening his office for business. Magda was the only person he allowed to distract him from his self-imposed isolation. With time, even Magda wasn't enough to dissipate his anger and rebellion. However, his withdrawal and resignation didn't last for long; momentous events beyond his control dictated an unforeseen trajectory.

THE SIX-DAY WAR

"**I** don't know where to send you," an officer told David when he presented himself to the military headquarter at the Cairo suburb of Helmeyah where all the reserve recruits were processed. "Why don't you take your summons to the medical corps and let them assign you to wherever they need you?" The officer advised him.

It was late in May 1967 when David received that summons. A new crisis was brewing in the Middle East for a few weeks when Israel had amassed its military forces at the border with Syria in response to Syrian bombardment of Israeli settlements below the Golan Heights. Egypt responded by closing the Tiran Strait at the Gulf of Aqaba to the Israeli ships and demanded the withdrawal of the United Nations Emergency Force. The UN Force was stationed at Sharm El Sheikh, the strategic location where the Gulf of Aqaba and the Gulf of Suez diverged to enclose the V-shaped Sinai Peninsula, to enforce the ceasefire agreement and guarantee the safe passage of Israeli ships through the Strait after the 1956 War. The stage was thus set for a certain war with Israel. Nasser, accordingly, ordered complete mobilization of the Egyptian army and moved the bulk of Egypt's military forces to Sinai.

David, with the summons in his hand, went to the army's medical headquarters at Manshiat El Backry, another district of Cairo famous for the presence of the personal residence of Gamal Abdel Nasser, a military hospital, and military barracks and headquarters. Once more, he received the same response. "They have recalled hundreds of doctors, and we don't have a place for all of you," an officer told him. "I suggest that you stay at home until we know where to send you."

This doesn't bode well for the coming war, David thought as he was leaving the building. Suddenly, he stopped at the exit as if struck by lightning. *What if they don't call me at home?* That possibility crossed his mind. In that case, he would be considered a deserter, a frightening eventuality. He reentered the building, determined to know his fate, right then and there. He remembered that his friend Hassan, who had joined the military, had an office in that building, and David wisely sought his help.

"David?" Hassan greeted him with apparent surprise. "Did they recall you?"

"Yes," he said.

David quickly told his friend the details of what had transpired. He concluded by saying, "I don't want to be considered a deserter if I get lost in this mess."

Hassan reassured him that he would work immediately on finding a suitable position for him in one of the military hospitals. After a few telephone calls and consultations with colleagues, Hassan found a place for his friend in a field hospital at the front line in Sinai.

"Sorry my friend, I couldn't arrange for something less dangerous. You don't mind going to the front line?" Hassan asked.

"No." The answer was quick and clear. David knew that being in the reserve force wouldn't entitle him to a privileged place anywhere west of the Suez Canal. If he had to be in a war, the front line, where his surgical skills would be needed the most, seemed to be a logical and welcomed choice. This war would be different. He knew that a war against a real army with modern weapons would certainly inflict a large number of casualties and injuries, nothing like the Yemen war where his surgical skills were hardly needed.

"This war is going to be a breeze," Hassan said as he was finalizing the paperwork. To reassure him further, he opened the *Al-Ahram* newspaper to an article by its chief editor, Hassanein Heikal, the acknowledged confidant of Nasser. "Look at the analysis of Heikal," Hassan said. "The numbers he quotes make the superiority of the Egyptian army clearly obvious. We have much more soldiers, airplanes, tanks, and guns. Heikal is a close friend of Nasser, and he must have an insider's information. He predicts an easy and quick victory."

David wasn't sure about that. He learned not to trust the official pronouncements. Even if the numbers were correct, and he had no reason to doubt their accuracy, his experience in the Yemen war diminished his trust in the fighting capabilities of the Egyptian army, especially with its antiquated equipments, obsolete WWII tactics, and the questionable competence of its commanders. However, he had to dismiss his doubts very quickly, as the confident and joyous atmosphere around him left no room for pessimism. Victory was never in doubt. Hassan reinforced that certainty with a personal touch to comfort his friend.

"Actually, the field hospital you're joining is already in place near Al-Areesh, just a few kilometers from your old town," he said. "In a few days, you'll find yourself in your birth place of Al Lodd."

David became overcome by nostalgia as he heard the name of Al Lodd. He imagined himself walking the streets of his childhood's town with all his senses attuned to its sights and smells. *Was it possible,* he wondered, *that he would see his old home again, his old schoolmates, the main street, and the train station?* However, when he recalled the first time he became aware of the Palestinian problem in that fateful day of 1948 and the subsequent war in 1956, his nostalgic mood quickly disappeared. Nothing had changed since then. The same religious battles, the same racial conflicts, and the same nationalistic wars were still raging and tearing the whole region apart. How could that have happened in the land that produced the Prophet of Peace? Were all prophets a fraud, preaching love and forgiveness, when they actually induced hatred and deadly conflicts? His intellectual wandering came to an end when the voice of Hassan brought him back to reality.

"Here is your free, first-class train ticket," Hassan was saying. "I'll cable your unit to have someone at the train station in Al-Areesh to take you to your unit. I am giving you three days to prepare yourself before you head to Sinai. Good luck."

The train slowly pulled out of Cairo until it cleared the northern edge of the expanding metropolis where it picked up speed to cross the Sharkeyah Province on the eastern side of the Delta. David watched the green fields as each one successively receded from his sight. Peasants, with ragged clothes and the same primitive tools that were used since the time of the pharaohs, were laboring peacefully on their farms, as if the looming war was somebody else's business and not theirs. There he was, the eternal Egyptian Fellah, tending his land as he did for thousands of years while his rulers were deciding his destiny without any regard to his opinion. *Could it be,* David thought, *that this time around Egyptians would abandon their passivity in favor of aggressiveness and conquest, as had happened during the reign of the Pharaoh Tuhotmos whose armies drove the Heksos out of Egypt and advanced up to Asia Minor? Isn't that the same aggressiveness and conquest that also drove the Europeans to innovate and dominate the whole world? After all, the revolutionary changes in human history weren't accomplished by sedentary and established societies, but by aggressive, risk-taking invaders we call barbarians.*

At Ismailia, the train approached the Suez Canal to take a northerly course along its western side. A few kilometers south of Kantara Gharb, it crossed the Ferdan Bridge on its way to the new train station in Kantara Shark, where it backed up slowly to enter the dead-end station.

When David stepped onto the platform, he found out that his train was not going to continue its trip beyond Kantara; civilian trains were not allowed into the soon-to-be battlefield. He was told to go to the old train station to resume his trip in a military train. He crossed the customhouse and stood next to the horse-drawn carriages that lined up across from the familiar quarantine waiting patiently for potential customers. A gentle, salty breeze drew his attention to the direction of the canal on his left side. A ferry blew its siren as it started to cross the canal. He was about to scream Eva's name, as he saw, in his mind's eye, her specter sitting down in the ferry, as had happened some distant years earlier. But he forcefully held his breath until his lungs were about to explode. Finally, he exhaled with a sorrowful, long sound that carried no name or any other word. Although more scientific reasoning had already replaced his old beliefs in vibrations, extrasensory perception, telepathy, and such pseudoscientific thinking, those old beliefs resurfaced in desperation, as if he were holding onto a straw to save him from his own despondency. Mysteriously, the apparition of Eva remained vivid in his mind. Everything around him disappeared in a transcendental trance with nothing to feel, see, hear, or touch except his beloved Eva. He silently told her how much he loved her, missed her, and needed her in that despairing moment. If he survived that war, he promised to find her wherever she might be. Somehow, he became reassured that Eva would receive his message. Soon, a peaceful serenity descended upon him and brought him back to reality. He headed to the first carriage in line.

"Welcome, honorable officer," the carriage driver greeted him. "It will be my pleasure to take you to the old train station."

The driver appeared to be in a talkative mood. He clearly wanted to express his political views and his own opinions about the coming war, in an explicit attempt to engage his passenger in the politics of the Middle East. But David was in no mood to start a conversation. He was more interested in watching the military convoys that shared the road with his carriage as the usual chaos he was familiar with drew his attention. Nothing had changed. His heart sank as the possibility of defeat crossed his mind. He was deeply absorbed in his own musings, when a statement from the driver startled him and dislodged his wandering thoughts.

"God willing, our army will triumph against the Jews, the Christians, the infidels, and the enemies of Islam." That's what the carriage driver had said.

David didn't want to believe his ears. What he had just heard must have been the opinion of one uneducated, fanatic, ignorant driver. But was it? He wondered, as he recalled the inflammatory songs and pronouncements that filled the airwaves, especially from the "Voice of the Arabs," the ultra-nationalistic radio station. The famous announcer, Ahmad Said, had already declared the inevitable triumph of the faithful army of God. Inflammatory songs, hastily composed with trashy words and primitive music, called for death, blood, killing, and destruction of the infidels. He couldn't help but compare all that to the German music and culture that helped the German nation to decisively dominate most of Europe in the first few years of World War II. Yes, Germany was ultimately defeated, but only by a more superior scientific and humanistic culture that was essentially influenced by the same elevating German music, methodical science, and progressive thinking. His Jewish neighbors in Palestine and Egypt listened to that same music of Beethoven and Wagner, practiced that same science, and believed in that same thought. However the whole Arabic world was still holding on to medieval thinking and an ancient way of life, anaesthetized by melancholic music and songs of dejection, loss, and unfulfilled love. When he recalled that Om Kolthoom, the most popular Egyptian singer, was about to perform before an impending war in one of her monthly concerts that usually last for hours and listened to by mostly hashish-smoking listeners throughout the whole Arabic world, he speculated on which party would win the war. To his dismay, the answer was obvious.

The old train station was swarmed with all ranks of military personnel, and a long train was being loaded with military wares. David found out that it would be a few hours before the train would leave the station. So he walked the streets of his old city, absent-mindedly, as if in a daze, until he found himself in the British cemetery. He sat down under the eucalyptus tree that witnessed his meetings with Eva, their first embrace, their first kiss, and their farewells. He felt grateful that Eva was safely somewhere away from the sure-to-come war. He only hoped that he would survive and succeed in immigrating to the United States. That was his only chance of finding Eva, even if that seemed to be close to impossible. Somehow, he knew deep in his heart that he would find her once he moved outside the restrictive shackles of Egypt. Getting out of Egypt became an obligation and obsession, not just a desire.

When he finally boarded the train, he remembered his last trip out of Palestine in 1948. Now he was crossing the Sinai Desert in a reverse direction, as if history was unfolding backward in front of him. Could it be possible that he would see Al Lodd again? He sincerely wanted to believe in the optimism of the Egyptian army and the assured victory just to relive his childhood's memories. However, his pessimistic assessment ultimately prevailed.

To his great disappointment, nobody was waiting for him at the Al-Areesh Train Station. He had to hitchhike a ride in a military truck to his destination.

The chief doctor greeted him as he entered the small field hospital. "Did you have a pleasant trip?" The chief doctor asked.

"Actually," David said in a reproachful voice, "I expected to find someone waiting for me at the train station."

"Do you mean that nobody was waiting for you?"

'No. I had to hitchhike a ride to get here."

"That is ridiculous. I told the supply officer to send a car for you. I'll find out what happened. Please accept my apologies."

"No apologies are necessary. The hitchhiking turned out to be a valuable learning experience. It reminded me of previous similar incidents."

"We'll talk about that in the future," the chief Doctor said. "But for now, let me introduce you to the rest of our doctors and take you on a tour through our hospital."

The field hospital was attached to an army division stationed near Al-Areesh. No less than a dozen doctors from different specialties formed the core of the hospital staff. A fully equipped operating room, with two adjoining operating tables, was set in one corner of the building. That's where the tour started, as David was supposed to join the surgeons who were responsible for running the operating room. The tour ended in the living quarters, which included an officers' mess, a comfortable recreation room, and a cleanly furnished sleeping area—a far cry from the miserable quarters he lived in during the Yemen War.

An air base was located a few kilometers away, where fighter planes were frequently seen taking off and landing in apparent pre-war maneuvers. The mighty display of the Egyptian military power gave David reassurance, and he soon fell back into a daily routine. He took his turn with the other doctors in seeing patients at the outpatient clinic. What interested him more were his daily encounters with the active military officers, who congregated in the hospital at the end of each day to play cards, listen to Om Kolthoom, or discuss the issues of the upcoming war. The mood was jubilant, optimistic, and confident of Egypt's assured victory. These were military people who were not in need of Haikal's opinion to comfort them, David reassured himself. These were the confidant executioners of the coming war.

Around seven on the morning of June 5, David was shaving his face when he heard the sound of airplanes flying above his room. He went out expecting to see the daily fighters' maneuvers. However, what he saw were low-flying airplanes, not the high-flying ones he was accustomed to, heading toward the nearby airbase. They were flying so low that he thought he could touch them if he were to raise his hands in the air. The cloudless sky was brilliantly blue, and the early morning air was suffused with the freshness of the desert around him. Nothing seemed to be unusual. *These must be Egyptian planes practicing low flying,* he thought. He returned to his room to finish shaving when a nearby explosion brought him back to the outside. Mushroom clouds were rising up toward the sky from the direction of the airbase. A second explosion brought out the chief doctor, who stood there wondering about the cause of these explosions. Everything around them seemed to be normal; soldiers were busy with their daily chores as if nothing was happening.

"One of the airplanes must have crashed." David voiced his thoughts. However, the chief doctor knew better; he looked at another wave of low flying airplanes and declared that they were Israeli planes.

"The war has started," the chief doctor pronounced. "These are Israeli planes, attacking our airbase."

"But why didn't our anti-aircraft artillery shoot them down? They are flying too low that you could have shot them with a rifle."

"Exactly," the chief doctor answered. "Because they are flying that low, they were not detected by our radar. But don't worry. Our commanders must have prepared for this scenario. Our air force should be able to absorb a first strike. Very soon, you will see our fighter planes filling the skies and our army advancing toward Israel. Let's prepare our hospital for the coming battles."

Back inside, the announcements from Radio Cairo were coming in full blast from portable radios. The assessment of the chief doctor seemed to be correct—a military communiqué acknowledged a surprise Israeli first strike but reassured the listeners that the Egyptian forces were finally engaged in the long-awaited battle with Israel. Actually, the communiqué declared that Egypt had downed forty Israeli planes. As the day progressed, radio broadcasts described ferocious battles as the Egyptian army was advancing inside Israel. More downed Israeli planes were gradually added to the list until the figure reached over 150. The military communiqués were periodically updated, while vitriolic pronouncements from Ahmad Said called for blood and killing and destruction.

David wanted to believe those broadcasts, but looking around him, he didn't see any army marching toward Israel. To his surprise, the commander of his military unit suddenly appeared at the door of the hospital to give an order for retreat toward the Suez Canal. Already, some army units were heading south, but this apparent retreat was clearly impeded by Israeli aerial attacks that forced the soldiers to abandon their vehicles when no Egyptian airplanes came to their rescue.

"I need trucks to haul my equipment and personnel to execute the evacuation order," the chief doctor told his military superior. "I also need protection. You can see for yourself how the Israeli airplanes are attacking any moving thing."

"My friend," the military commander said, "I can't even protect my own troops. You are on your own."

An approaching Israeli mechanized unit appeared at the horizon at that moment. A few shells were fired at the approaching unit, but a barrage of bullets from a low-flying Israeli airplane silenced any further resistance. Soon enough, the Israeli unit was in full control of the whole position. Egyptian soldiers were allowed to walk away, but the officers were rounded up and taken as prisoners of war. They were packed in a truck and sent back to Israel.

When the truck finally stopped, David descended with the other officers into what appeared to be a vast military barracks. Beyond a barbed-wire fence, he could see Mediterranean cypresses, olive trees, and expanses of green fields.

This was the land of his childhood, the land that witnessed religious wars since biblical times. *How many more wars would it take for humans to realize the futility of it all?* He wondered. The old prophets had certainly failed to bring peace. Maybe humanity was in need of a new breed of prophets different than the Biblical and Koranic ones, without any rigid dogma or ideology and with a universal human inclusiveness.

He stood in line to be registered like all the other POWs. When his turn came around, he gave his name and rank, and then he followed an Israeli guard to a ward where he collapsed on one of the neatly aligned beds. A radio broadcast in the Arabic language was transmitting the Israeli side of the war. He listened as the broadcaster announced the complete annihilation of the Egyptian air force and the capture of Al-Areesh. The Israeli army was on its way to the Suez Canal. As much as he didn't want to believe those reports, the evidence he saw led him to doubt the Egyptian communiqués he had listened to from Radio Cairo earlier on that long and fateful day. The following morning the broadcasts announced the capture of more Egyptian territory and the scattering of the Egyptian forces all over Sinai. More days brought more bad news, which he still refused to believe until the sixth day of the war when the voice of Nasser was broadcasted from the Israeli radio, calling for a ceasefire and announcing his resignation. The whole depth of the calamity finally sank in. Some prisoners had transistor radios, around which they gathered to listen to Radio Cairo. The news from Radio Cairo gave credence to what had already been broadcasted from Israel. No censorship was necessary as the news of the events of June 9 and 10 were flooding all radio waves. Nasser was, indeed, resigning from the office of the president of Egypt.

To the incredulous Egyptians, the resignation of Nasser left no doubt about the enormity of the defeat and the loss of Sinai. Paradoxically, instead of holding Nasser accountable for the unexpected outcome of the war, which he promised to win, Egyptians swarmed into the streets of Cairo and camped without food or sleep in utter despair, asking Nasser to stay. Next day, the drama ended when Nasser withdrew his resignation and accepted the demands of the masses to stay as their president. Thus the war ended as dramatically as it had started.

But it wasn't over for the Egyptian POWs; they found themselves fighting a psychological war waged against them by the Israeli propaganda machine. Israeli broadcasts dismissed Nasser's claim that Egypt had lost a battle, not the war, and proclaimed the annexation of the conquered territories into Israel proper, fulfilling the Biblical prophesies. David and the rest of the POWs patiently endured their captivity by the hope that Egypt would have had captured even a few Israeli combatants to allow for an orderly exchange of prisoners of war.

One day before the official end of the war, David was summoned to the office of the camp commander. He was ushered into a room where an Israeli officer was seated behind a small desk. Another Israeli officer, who was sitting across from the desk, stood up as David entered the room and shook his hand in a friendly gesture.

"I am Doctor Yosef," he said in a perfect Egyptian dialect. "This is Mosha, the commander of this camp. There is no need for formalities, so let me go directly to the issue at hand. A few kilometers from here, there is a hospital at which I am the only surgeon. We are getting more casualties from Sinai, mostly Egyptians. Our military made it clear that they can't spare another doctor to send here."

David immediately realized what that introduction was leading to. "Well, that's your problem," he said. "You are winning the war, so deal with its consequences."

Although he had no idea of his legal rights and obligations, he knew that he wouldn't cooperate with the enemy and be stigmatized as a traitor. He glanced at the direction of the commander, who was still sitting behind his desk, but appeared to be intently following their conversation. The commander slowly stood up and took a few steps toward David.

"You're absolutely right," he said in English. "However, due to the fact that we are getting a large number of casualties from the front, we do need your help, at least for the sake of your compatriots. I know a lot about you. You are a competent surgeon and an educated, reasonable human being. You are also not in the active service, and you may not be cognizant of international laws.

Let me reassure you that you wouldn't be called a collaborator just by helping us give the required medical care to POWs. Actually, article thirty-two of the Geneva Convention, which deals with the treatment of prisoners of war, clearly states that POWs from the medical profession may be required by the detaining power to exercise their medical function in the interest of the POWs."

"Well," David said, "I don't doubt what you have just told me. Before I make a decision, I have to ask my senior officer for his permission."

"Absolutely," the Israeli commander said. "Yosef will go with you to meet your commanding officer. I am sure that he will not have any objections."

The Egyptian commanding officer readily gave his consent. He was actually pleased that an Egyptian doctor would be giving medical care to Egyptian casualties. On their way back, David found out that he would be moved to the nearby hospital where he would be accorded the same privileged living arrangements as his Israeli counterparts, a welcome change from the prison-like existence in the POW camp.

His work started immediately as casualties were brought to the hospital in a steady stream. He had to do his own triage and start operating on the more serious injuries. An adequately equipped operating room and competent nursing staff were under his disposition. Yosef operated in an adjoining operating room and shared in the post-operative care. However, the flow of casualties, thankfully, started to trickle in a matter of days. By then, David had found out that most individuals of the retreating army either made it back to Egypt on foot or, if their injuries were severe enough to obviate a walk back to Egypt, perished in the desolate desert.

Gradually, a professional camaraderie and a respectful friendship developed between the two doctors. During a casual conversation, David was surprised to know that Yosef was originally from Egypt and that he had attended his first year of medical school at Ein Shams, the second largest medical school in Cairo. After the 1956 War, he was expelled from Egypt with the other Egyptian Jews. He ended up in Israel where he finished his medical education. In his turn, the Israeli doctor was equally surprised when he knew that David was born in Al Lodd.

"David," Yosef said one day, "in a few days you'll be going back to Egypt. I have just learnt that an exchange of POWs is imminent. I will surely miss you. Anything I can do for you before you leave?"

David's life-long pursuit of Eva crossed his mind. Although it seemed a remote possibility, he decided to give it a try. His extrasensory perception returned with an unexplainable force and a hopeful anticipation.

"Actually," he said, "you might. I happened to know a Jewish Egyptian girl who had left Egypt in '56 like you. She was a student at the Faculty of Liberal Arts at that time, but she was with me in the same elementary school when we were growing up in Kantara."

Could she be the Eva he knew? Yosef wondered when he heard the word *Kantara.* She did grow up in Kantara, but she didn't have a liberal arts background as David had told him; this Eva was a doctor. There was one way to find out.

"Is her name Eva by any chance?" Yosef asked.

Hearing her name was like a thunderbolt that struck David so violently that the blood drained out of his face. Yosef thought that his friend was about to go into shock. He stretched him flat on the floor and started to measure his blood pressure and pulse rate. The flat position revived David in a short time. He shook his head as if recovering from a dream and looked at Yosef in disbelief.

"Did I hear you correctly? Did you mention the name, Eva?" He asked.

Yosef nodded.

"Yes, yes. She must be the one. Do you know her?"

"Yes, I do. It happened that she is a good friend of my wife. They were in the same medical school in Tel Avid before Eva went to New York to finish the rest of her medical education. Actually, she has been recalled back to Israel and is serving now with my wife in a nearby hospital."

Reluctant to reveal too much information to an Israeli, even one as friendly as Yosef, David withheld details of his relationship with Eva. After all, she might have gotten married and forgotten all about him.

"It's a true miracle to find her after so many years." That's all he could say. "How can I see her?" He asked.

"My wife is supposed to visit me tomorrow. I'll call and ask her to bring Eva with her."

The gods, if there were gods, must be on his side. And his extrasensory perception was correct, David thought. Every time circumstances separated him from Eva, something good happened to bring them back together. The move to Cairo that disjointed them for the first time turned out to be a temporary barrier that disappeared when Eva managed to let her parents send her to the university. Even her parents' divorce that was supposed to deliver her into the custody of her father and the restrictive Muslim law, which would have been a formidable obstacle to overcome, had transformed her into a more approachable Jew. And now, the seemingly unbridgeable divide that had separated them for the previous eleven years appeared to be coming to an end. When the possibility that Eva might have stopped loving him or that she was married to another man crossed his mind, he became dejected and couldn't fall asleep that night. When he finally dozed at dawn, a vision of Eva appeared to him. The apparition didn't say a word, but her smiling face, wrapped in divine light, seemed to transmit a message of reassurance and comfort. When he woke up, he felt nothing of his previous anxiety. Somehow, he was sure that the gods would never disappoint him. He was ready to see Eva, touch her, talk to her, and face the facts, whatever they turned out to be.

LOST AND FOUND

Eva was doing her residency training at the New York University Hospital in New York City when the Israeli government recalled her as a reservist, a few weeks before the start of the war. Because of her connection to Yosef and his wife, she asked, and was granted an assignment with them in the field hospitals. Her fluency in the Egyptian dialect, similar to her two friends, was a good reason to post her close to the Egyptian border. When Yosef's wife invited her for a visit to Yosef's hospital, she hadn't the faintest idea of what was waiting for her.

"Oh, my God," Eva screamed as she entered the room and saw David standing next to Yosef. "This couldn't be true," she said, as her knees started to buckle.

David rushed to her side and supported her body just before she was about to hit the floor. In his arms, she gradually regained her strength and balance. She held David's face with her two hands and took a step backward to look into his eyes.

"Tell me it is true. Tell me it is you in person and not in a dream," she said.

"It is true, Eva," he said.

When David tried to kiss her, she withdrew from his embrace and reflexively looked at his hand, as if a dreadful thought had crossed her mind. She gave a sigh of relief when she didn't find a wedding ring on his finger. However, clarification of another issue was necessary before she would completely surrender to him.

"Then tell me," she said, "Why didn't you answer my letters?"

"What letters?"

"I have sent you many letters from Israel and New York."

"I didn't receive any letters from you," he said. And then, as if a revelation had dawned on him, he added: "Your letters must have been confiscated by the Egyptian censors. They are notorious for their diligence when it comes to foreign mail. However, I didn't need any letters to keep my promise and stay wholesome for you. You were always in my heart, in my mind, and in every drop of my blood."

"This explains everything. I am beginning to see things clearly," she said.

Her overflowing emotions stopped her from saying anything else. Instead, she hugged him and kissed him and finally rested her head on his shoulder as tears of joy streamed from her eyes. When she collected her composure, she wiped her eyes and stepped back.

"Oh, David," she said, "I know now that my waiting wasn't in vain. Somehow I believed all the time that I was bound to see you again. That's why I remained wholesome for you, too."

They hugged and kissed again and again until they heard some noise from Josef's direction. They looked at each other and then suddenly exploded with laughter when they simultaneously remembered another interruption to their open expression of love during a felucca excursion on the Nile. This time, though, there was no threat on their lives and they saw no need to hide their emotions from their two friends. They remained in each other embrace.

"Remember, David, when we used to talk about vibrations and telepathy?" Eva said. "Well, I have felt vivid vibrations, especially lately, as if you were calling my name. You too must have felt similar vibrations as I was always calling your name. Tell me that you have heard my voice. You must have, or else why you didn't you get married?"

David recounted what he had experienced just a few days earlier standing next to the Suez Canal and sitting under the eucalyptus tree at the English cemetery in Kantara.

"Eva," he finally said. "There were more incidents like these ones. I have always believed that we would be together again. That's why I have kept my vows and overcome all the troubles I have encountered."

"I can understand what you are telling me. I had the same experiences and managed to survive through my own pains and trials. Fate has been cruel to us. From now on, we must control our own destiny and prevent fate from dictating our future."

They continued to talk in this manner as if they had regained the innocence of their youth. Finally, a lot of catching up became necessary. Eva told him about her escape from Egypt, her arrival to Israel, her decision to become a doctor, and her subsequent emigration to America.

At the end, she said, "A major disadvantage of being an Israeli citizen is that all Israeli reservists are liable to be recalled to serve from wherever they are in the world, although that turned out to be in our advantage."

"You didn't have to wait for a war to come back. You could have come to Egypt when you were free to do so from America."

"I tried, but the Egyptian consulate refused to give me a visa on my Israeli passport. Remember, I am not an American citizen yet. I do not have an American passport."

While Yosef and his wife listened with obvious interest, David and Eva didn't stop talking. David asked about her mother, but she appeared to be reluctant to say much about her. All she said was that her mother had married an Israeli and was currently living with him in Tel Aviv.

When it was David's turn, he told her about his medical school, his residency years, and his medical practice in Cairo. He expanded on his experience in Yemen and on how he saw the Yemen War as a harbinger for Egypt's defeat in the Six-Day War. When Eva asked about what he did in Cairo beside studying and working, he understood what was behind that question. He carefully described the cultural and intellectual circles he was involved with, but he made sure to avoid mentioning Magda and the Russian girls.

Yosef and his wife listened silently to the surprising revelations, when suddenly a grimace contorted Eva's face, as if she remembered something awful.

"Is it true that Israel had agreed on a prisoners' exchange?" She directed her question to Yosef.

"Yes. Actually this will happen in a matter of days."

"I don't believe it," she said as she looked at David with an aggrieved expression. "The minute I find you, they take you away from me. I hate the whole Middle East. But this time, we'll never be separated again."

Yosef looked inquisitively at David, who found it necessary to explain. "Back when we were young," David said, "we had a dream to go to America where our different religions wouldn't be an issue as they were in Egypt. Eva has managed to go to America already. It is now my turn to join her."

"Exactly," Eva said. "Soon I will return to America. I will send you an Affidavit of Support from there, which will make it easy for you to get an American visa. This time around, as I won't trust the Egyptian censors, I'll find someone traveling to Egypt to deliver it to you personally."

One thing remained to be settled. She looked at Yosef's wife and said, "How come you didn't tell me who the Egyptian doctor was when you invited me come here and meet him?"

"I didn't know anything about the whole thing," her friend said.

"Neither did I," Yosef joined in. "Actually, I knew nothing about your fascinating story. I thought that you were only good friends. Now I understand why Eva didn't get married or have a relationship with another man. Eva, I thought you were waiting for a prince on a white horse. Now I know who the prince is."

"You were about to kill me by this surprise. But I forgive you, Yosef. I would have happily accepted anything just to see David again."

It was late in the evening when Eva and Yosef's wife returned to their unit. Eva made sure that she had David's correct address in Cairo, and repeated her promise to write when she went back to New York. They hugged and kissed and laughed and cried and didn't want to leave each other. Yosef's wife had to pull Eva away, reminding her that she had to go back to her unit. The inevitability of another separation became obvious. However, this time around a resolution was in sight, and David finally relaxed his grip on Eva's body, even though he kept holding her hand.

"Yosef," Eva said, as she turned her head to look back, "I am glad that you have become such good friends." She withdrew her hand from David's, gave him a final kiss, and departed with Yosef's wife.

…

It was in Nicosia Airport in Cyprus that the POW exchange took place. During the flight out of Israel, David was reading a *Der Spiegel* article in the English translation given to him by Yosef. When he had finished reading it, he gave it to the chief doctor, who was sitting next to him.

The article explained the reason behind the spectacular success of the first Israeli air strike. As most of the Israeli airplanes were French Mirages with a flying range that would not allow them to reach deep into Egypt, Israel solved that impediment by adding an extra fuel tank to the Mirages. To compensate for the extra weight, they had to lighten the load of ammunition, which required fewer weapons but with more accuracy and effectiveness. The Israeli engineers designed a special bomb to disable the Egyptian runways in a first strike. It was a bomb that would initially bore into the runway and then explode underground to create a large crater, making the runway unfit for takeoff and landing. What was left for the execution of a surprise attack was to evade the Egyptian radar. To do that, all Israeli pilots practiced on low flying under the radar screen.

'What do you think of these reports?" David asked his chief doctor.

"They make me sick."

"Is it not strange that foreign newspapers know more about our enemy than we do?"

"Don't underestimate our intelligence," the chief doctor replied. "I have been in the active military service long enough to trust them. This was a deceptive enemy who took us by surprise. We would have prevailed if there was no surprise."

"But that's the point. Wars are all about deception and surprises," David said.

"We know that," the chief doctor said. "We have our surprises too. The Russians will replace all the airplanes and arms we lost in this war. I have confidence that Nasser will rebuild our army and ultimately win the war with Israel. I believe him when he says that we lost a battle, not the war."

"I assume that you don't hold him responsible for this defeat," David said.

"It is the military commanders who lost this war, not him."

"But he is the one who chose those commanders," David persisted. "He should have tested their competency and expertise."

"He did. These are the same people who helped him in his successful revolution."

"Then you agree with the masses that converged in the streets of Cairo in the hundreds of thousands begging him to withdraw his resignation and stay in office."

"Of course, he is the only person who can turn this defeat into a victory," the chief doctor maintained, "as he did in other conflicts since the beginning of the revolution."

"I hope that you're right, but I have my own doubts."

"My advice is that you should keep your doubts to yourself. Even talking to someone like me can put you in grave danger. I assure you that I am not to be feared as an informer, but you never know who is spying on us just now."

David realized the validity of the chief doctor's warning; he never discussed politics again.

When he reached Cairo, he became determined to leave the country as soon as he could. A letter from Eva, delivered to him by a friend of hers from New York, made his decision possible.

"Dearest David:

"Our far-fetched but blessed meeting at the POW camp makes me believe in our unavoidable destiny. I was in utter despair when I didn't receive any response to my letters. Now I know better; I am sending this letter with an American friend who is going to Egypt and will deliver it to you personally.

"David, my life hasn't been easy since my parents' divorce. I don't want to bother you with too many details, but I'll explain everything when you join me in New York.

"You can imagine my joy when I found myself in America; half of our plan had been accomplished. The first thing I was determined to do, once I got my American passport, was to go back to Egypt and search the whole country until I found you. But getting the passport will take two more years, and I can't wait that much longer. Hurry, my love, and come to America as soon as you can. The enclosed Affidavit of Support should help you get an American visa immediately. It is now your turn to get out of Egypt and complete our dream. I'll be waiting for you.

"My love, you remember our discussions about energy, vibrations, and telepathy? Well, you have been with me through the last few years, despite the long distance and time that separated us. Before I saw you at the POW camp, I always had a premonition that I would meet you again. Maybe that's why it was easy for me to keep my vow and remain wholesome for you. When I saw you in Israel—sorry, Palestine—and discovered that you weren't married, I knew that your vibrations were in harmony with mine. Isn't that what you used to tell me?

"My love, it is time for both of us to rescue ourselves from the turbulent Middle East. We have suffered enough from the ignorance and intolerance of its people. America is a wonderful country where we can live together. My life will never be complete until you come and be permanently with me. If you want to know how much I love you, just read Elizabeth Browning's poem, 'How do I Love Thee.' I might have written it myself.

"Your loving Eva."

He wrote an answer to her letter, which he gave to her American friend before he left Egypt.

"Dearest Eva:

"What a joy it was to receive your letter! Now that I have found you, nothing will stand in my way to join you in America. I expect my visa to the US to be coming soon.

"Your extra sensory perception is absolutely correct. My vibrations are indeed in harmony with yours, and your love is the only thing that has kept me alive. I breathe, I eat, and I survive only on the hope of seeing you again.

"As you have correctly said, we have been separated by the suffocating culture of the Middle East, and then by the long distance and time that were forced upon us. Now that we have found each other, nothing will separate us again. I have already seen the fruits of freedom in the new direction of your life. Free together, we'll fulfill the rest of our childhood dreams. Nothing will stand in our way anymore. We'll be able to marry and live with each other permanently and forever.

"I don't know if we should use the regular mail; I don't trust the Egyptian censors. I have befriended a clerk in the American Embassy who helped me with the visa application. He provided me with his telephone number and promised to take care of our correspondence. Call his number and arrange with him a convenient time to talk with me. Nothing will make me happier than hearing your voice.

"I love you eternally. David."

To David's good luck, Nasser loosened his iron grip on the Egyptians. Although the government still suppressed open dissent, it allowed the dissenters to leave the country. By the time his American visa was issued, David had already obtained a discharge from the army. With the American visa secured, a passport and exit visa, as required by the Egyptian law, became possible. He left the country before the end of the 1967- fateful year.

When he boarded the airplane at the Cairo Airport, he had only one hundred dollars in his pocket, as no one was allowed to leave with more than that amount. But his invaluable treasure was a photograph of Eva, which she had sent him in her last letter and that he had looked at a million times before his airplane landed at John F. Kennedy International Airport in New York City.

NEW YORK

As soon as David stepped into the arrival hall of JFK in New York, he spotted Eva standing among the waiting crowd.

"Eva!" he shouted.

"David!" she screamed.

She ran to him and threw herself into his open arms. Each one started to talk at the same time, as if it was more urgent to talk than to listen. "I love you. I miss you," they uttered the same words, almost simultaneously, more from a compulsive intent to express their overflowing emotions than to listen to the other. They laughed, cried, and embraced amid a jumble of words until the urgency to talk had subsided. She stepped back and held his head between her extended hands and showered his face with kisses until her lips found his. He reflexively disengaged from her burning lips and looked at the surrounding crowd with apparent embarrassment. When his body tensed in her embrace, she understood what was going on in his mind. She looked at him with a frowning expression.

"David," she said. Her voice was more sarcastic than surprised. "We are not in Egypt. We are in a free country, and I can openly hug you and kiss you and love you without fear or embarrassment. Isn't that what we were dreaming of?"

"Yes, yes," he said. "Maybe I still have some unresolved inhibitions, considering what had happened to us at Al Kanater Al Khaireya."

"I still remember that scene, but I overcame it once I left Egypt," she said. "You will do the same after you experience the freedom that the whole world seems to enjoy."

She held his hand and led him out of the arrival hall.

"We have a lot to talk about, but let's first walk to the parking lot," she continued. "I have waited eleven years to have you beside me, and I can surely wait for a few more minutes to avenge the cruelty of the Middle East that had separated us for so long. You won't be embarrassed when I lock you in my apartment and show you how much I love you."

"Oh, my love," he said, "you don't know how much I wanted to hug you and kiss you the minute I saw you, but you just have to give me some time to get rid of my old conditioned reflexes. After all, I am the product of a conservative culture. Don't expect me to change in just one day."

"I understand," she said.

They were next to the car when he unexpectedly encircled her with his arms. Her body softened and responded to his every movement. Her eyes glistened and her emotions overflowed with joy as she reciprocated his affection. When he finally loosened his grip on her, it was her turn to pull out from his embrace.

"You're really a fast learner," she said.

She led the way to the rear of the car where he methodically put his suitcase in the trunk, walked around to the passenger's side, and sat down next to her before she drove out of the parking lot.

"Tell me about everything," he said, "from the moment you left the POW camp until now."

"But I have told you all that in my letters," she said. "There will be plenty of time to fill in the gaps."

She was so distracted by this conversation that she missed the ramp to the highway. She had to circle around the airport until she found her way to the Van Wyck Expressway. Her excitement, though, kept her talking.

"David," she said. "I guess you don't believe in predestination and the paranormal. But I believe that we were destined to meet at the POW camp by a mysterious power that had bound us to begin with. I always believed that we were fated to meet again despite the evidence to the contrary. This belief has kept me faithful to you. We'll discuss that later, but for now, why don't you tell me how you became involved in the Six-Day War? What happened before I saw you in the POW camp?"

He told her about his summons and his adventure with the military bureaucracy. He embellished on what he had told her previously about the horse-drawn carriage and its driver in Kantara and his visit to the English cemetery. He told her about the surprising Israeli strike. He ended up by summarizing the report he read in the *Der Spiegel* magazine. He contrasted that with her statement about predestination and the paranormal and concluded by saying that only the scientific method would ultimately determine the consequences of any cause-and-effect progression.

"You can't deny that religious beliefs played a major role in the outcome of this war; the Jews were driven by the biblical covenant with their God. Don't you think so?" she asked, accepting his challenge.

"Survival played the only part. Remember that the Jews were fighting for their survival. If your reasoning is correct, then how come that the religious beliefs of the Arabs didn't help them win the war? They have a similar backing from the same God. Survival is for the fittest, and the scientific method is the assured road for survival."

"You have a point," she said. "I am only teasing you."

"What!" he said, "I didn't expect you to give up that easily. You must have changed."

"Yes I did," she said. "Remember how you introduced me to science back in Cairo? You get credit for this change. Now that I am working in a scientific profession, I have a better grasp on how nature works. Oh, how I miss the discussions we had in Cairo! It is very hard and rare to have intelligent conversations here. People around me are more concerned with their daily survival than to think of intellectual abstractions. This is what I call the American survivalist mode—work, work, work."

Heavy traffic was building up that distracted her from pursuing her thoughts. "Survival dictates that I concentrate on the road," she said with a loud chuckle. "We'll have plenty of time to discuss these issues. In the meantime, let me be your tour guide and introduce my city to you. New York City consists of five boroughs…"

The traffic was hardly moving when they finally joined the long column of cars on the Van Wyck Expressway. It took them two hours to reach their destination in Manhattan. During that time, she continued her geography lesson, pointing to every landmark on the way.

"This is Jamaica Hospital on our left, a community hospital servicing the poorer areas of Queens. I am sure that its interns and residents get a tremendous experience from the wealth of pathology that must come their way. I'll show you Bellevue Hospital later on, the closest thing to Kasr El Eini in Cairo. That's where you should work. Of course, you have to pass the ECFM (Educational Council for Foreign Medical Graduates) exam first. It's a pity that they don't hold this exam in Egypt. It would have saved us a lot of valuable time if you had taken the exam before coming here. Now that you are here, however, I'll be able to familiarize you with the American medicine and the multiple-choice exams. It will be easy to grasp all that for someone with your knowledge and experience."

"Can I work without the ECFMG?" he asked.

"No," she answered. "Actually, you can't work here as a doctor unless you go through American training. You have to do a residency again, but only after you pass the ECFMG exam. I have already obtained an application for you. In the meantime, I am trying to get you a job in one of the smaller hospitals. This will not count toward your American training, but who cares? We have all the time in the world."

"I see that you have figured out everything," he said.

She didn't respond to his observation, as the converging traffic on the Grand Central Parkway demanded her full attention.

"It is a bottleneck here," she explained. "Many of the highways to New York City, mostly from Long Island, converge at this spot."

When she saw a long line of cars backed up on the exit ramp from the Grand Central Parkway to the Long Island Expressway and the Midtown Tunnel, she quickly veered to the left lane in the direction of Triborough Bridge. She aggressively merged onto the congested highway.

"This is worse than Cairo," she finally said. "But here, at least, there are alternative ways to your destination to choose from. Instead of the tunnel, I'll take you over a bridge to Manhattan. This is even better, as you will be able to see the skyline of New York. It is quite a sight to behold."

"What's that on my right?" He asked.

"Oh," she said. "This is the globe that was left over from the 1939 New York World's Fair. The area around it is Flushing Meadows, a large park with famous sports facilities. The stadium to your right is Shea Stadium."

She explained the game of baseball and then the American football, as she drove around La Guardia Airport. The merging traffic toward Triborough Bridge demanded her full attention and she stopped talking. From the top of the bridge, the skyline of Manhattan filled the view through the windshield. Very few clouds were scattered at the horizon, where the setting sun was coloring the western sky with a pallet of brilliant colors and spreading its fading light over and through the skyscrapers of Manhattan. She silently pressed his hand, as if to tell him that there was no need for her to explain the scenery or to express her emotions with words. They remained silent until they reached the East River Drive.

"Here we are in my city," she said, breaking the silence.

The southbound traffic was less congested at that time of the day. She thus returned to describing the city's landmarks. She continued as she drove down Second Avenue until they reached the corner of 23rd Street, where she parked her car in a garage under an apartment building.

"This is where I live," she said. "And this is where you will live with me. We'll never be separated again. I promise you."

He carried his suitcase to the elevator, along the corridor and into the apartment.

"Welcome to *our* home," she said as they stepped into the living room. "Come, unpack your suitcase." She led him to the bedroom and directed him to an empty closet. "I have emptied this closet for you."

Eva's place was a one-bedroom apartment on the fifteenth floor of a large building owned by the New York University Hospital, where she worked as a resident. Mostly residents, interns, nurses, and other hospital employees lived in that building. A full-size bed with a night table on each side and a dresser with a large mirror occupied most of the available space in the bedroom. Two spacious closets were enclosed in the adjoining walls, and a door opened into a modern bathroom. A living room of comfortable size accommodated a simple sitting area and a large wall unit packed with books and a complete stereo system with a receiver, a tape recorder, and a record player. A small dining table with four chairs took a corner of the space that was adjoining a small, well-equipped kitchen.

With great trepidation, David stepped into the bedroom as if he was entering a sacred temple. The room was spotlessly clean and smelled of an intoxicating feminine fragrance. He was tempted to take her to bed right then and there, but she seemed to intentionally avoid him.

"Don't you worry; I have a plan for the whole evening," she said. "You just go ahead and arrange your clothes in this closet and take a shower. By then I should have finished preparing our dinner. I have been waiting for you all those years, so let me do it my own way."

He saw the wisdom of her planning when he came out of the shower refreshed and vibrant, as if the stiffness from the long trip had been washed away under the hot water. As he passed the dresser, he noticed a half-empty pack of birth control pills, and he smiled. He splashed on his face some cologne he had bought from the duty-free shop, dressed in a clean shirt and pants, and stepped into the living room. The dining table was covered with a white tablecloth. A bouquet of red and yellow roses was arranged in an Egyptian alabaster vase, and a candle was lit on each side of it. Two complete dinner sets were placed on two adjoining sides of the table.

She came out of the kitchen and looked at him adoringly. Without speaking, she gave him a kiss on his cheek and then put a record on the turntable. The beginning chords of the Ninth Symphony filled the room with its hesitant first notes. She disappeared again into the kitchen, but soon enough reappeared with two glasses of red wine. She handed him one glass, kissed him again, and then raised her glass to touch his.

"This is to us, to our future, and to the triumphant joy of Beethoven's music."

"I drink to you, my love," he said as he raised his glass and took a sip of wine. "You have certainly thought of everything, including the most appropriate music for our first day together. But there must be something I can help you with."

"No," she said. "You are my guest today. Just sit down and enjoy the music until I finish preparing dinner. But don't worry. You'll have a lot of chores to do once I go back to work. I took this weekend off to familiarize you with the city and the American way of life. Once I go back to work on Monday, you'll be on your own. So enjoy yourself until then."

"I will," he said.

She took another sip of wine and resumed her explanation as she went in and out of the kitchen.

"I went through the shock of facing a different culture, a different country, and a different way of life. It wasn't easy for me, but I'll try to make it easier for you. We have lost too many years. Now that you are here, we have to go through a lot of catching up. Let's eat our dinner first before you get drunk with the wine. I want you to be sober for our first night together."

He understood the hint. He was thankful that he had taken a nap on the airplane, which was enough to keep him awake for another night. Fortunately, during his residency training, he learned how to take short naps, sitting down, which were enough to sustain him without sleep for days and nights on end.

After they had finished eating, she headed to the bedroom and started to undress. "You can clear the table and wash the dishes, while I take my shower," she said in a seductive voice before she crossed the threshold.

She was already under the sheets when he entered the bedroom. Her wet hair scattered in waves around her face. Her breasts looked like two solid mounds, and her nipples were well defined under the sheet. The outline of her body appeared to him like a marble sculpture, miraculously brought to life by a divine power. She looked at him with an inviting smile.

"Our time has arrived," she said. "Undress and come next to me."

Their naked bodies touched, and their pent-up desires exploded without restraint. They embraced, kissed, caressed each other, cried, and laughed. Then they rolled in bed until the inevitable act. He felt a virginal tightness that he had to overcome with ecstatic tenderness. He didn't stop, though, until they reached their climaxes together. Only then did he lift up his head and looked adoringly into her eyes.

"Eva," he said, "you are still a virgin!"

"Long time ago," she said, "in a British cemetery, I promised to keep myself wholesome for you. I have kept that promise. Thank heavens that you showed up before I lost my virginity to someone else! Now you know how much I love you."

His face radiated with happiness as he listened to her confession. However, this was soon replaced by a sad expression as he remembered the many women he had slept with, which made him realize how undeserving he was of the purity of her love. She instinctively guessed what was going on in his mind.

"David, don't feel guilty about your past," she said. "I am not that ignorant to dismiss the differences between men and women. I understand your needs and desires, and I wouldn't blame you if you had experiences before."

Without disengaging from each other, they had more desire to go at it for countless more times. They tried different positions and approaches until they had exhausted all their energies. When she rolled over to one side, he engaged her back with his body, stretched his hand around her chest to hold her breasts, buried his head in her soft hair, and the two of them surrendered to a contented sleep.

They were still in the same position, front to back, when he woke up the morning after. An exhilarating feeling swept through David as he experienced the joy of waking up with Eva in his arms for the first time in his life. And she wasn't any ordinary woman, a fact he was aware of all along. Her capacity for love wasn't ordinary either. The revelation of the previous night had shown him how deep her affection and sincere her commitments were.

He instinctively tightened his grip on her body, which made her open her eyes and turn around to face him with the most adoring smile.

"Good morning, David," she greeted him.

"Good morning, Eva," he responded as his lips searched for hers. The ensuing kiss led to a complete and intoxicating union that seemed to last forever. Utterly exhausted, they stayed in bed clinging to each other until their hearts returned to their normal beats and their breathing resumed a quieter rhythm. When he tried to kiss her again, she withdrew and jumped out of bed.

"Oh, no more," she laughingly said. "We can't stay in bed all day. Besides, I have planned a sightseeing tour for your first full day in my city. Get up. Let's take our showers."

He looked at her naked body as if he was seeing her for the first time. Her breasts were full and erect, defying the force of gravity, as if suspended by unseen threads. The chest and hips were well proportioned and elegantly defined by a slim waist. A flat abdomen and a straight back gave her a royal posture as she headed toward the bathroom. He couldn't help but follow her, mysteriously drawn to her by an irresistible force.

Their first shower together was another new experience that complemented and added to their intimacy. After she had finished rubbing his back, he took the Loofa—the fibrous, spongy, and traditional Middle Eastern body-scrubber—from her and scrubbed her entire body. He then used his hand to remove the soap and enjoy the smooth softness of her slippery skin. A kiss under the shower took them into a new domain, different from the ones they had experienced in their previous kisses. Reluctantly, they finally disengaged and stepped out of the shower. After drying each other's bodies, they dressed, had a quick breakfast, left the apartment, and exited the building to access the streets of New York.

"The best way to see New York," Eva said as they were out of the building, "is either to go up the Empire State Building or take the Circle Line for a three-hour cruise around Manhattan. Today, we'll do both. Of course, the third way is to walk, and I think we can start that by walking to the Empire State Building. This way, you can see more of the city."

And he did. All his senses sharpened to the sights and sounds and smells of the vibrant city. And he couldn't have asked for a better guide to introduce him to New York. From the observation deck of the Empire State Building, he marveled at the city grid as he saw it from that elevated perspective for the first time. An airplane happened to zoom across the sky, which made him marvel at the two of the unbelievable scientific accomplishments he was witnessing at that moment. The first was a large metal flying machine, defying the laws of gravity to rise above the Earth, what Aristotle called, "its natural home." And the other was a massive, elemental structure, ascending straight up without collapsing. He verbalized his wonder to Eva in an attempt to reinforce his previous opinions about the triumph of science. She was in no mood, though, to go through another intellectual argument; she had more pressing things to do in their first full day together. She told him to shut up and just enjoy the scenery.

Back on the street level, she led him uptown along Fifth Avenue. As they walked in front of the New York Public Library, she told him about the public library system in America and explained how it was easy to borrow books and research any subject he chose. She expanded on how much intellectual inquiries were sacred to the Americans, "All knowledge is available to anyone who seeks it," she said. "There is no censorship on the creative mind and no restrictions on the willing learner. This is what had produced the unique American innovations and technologies."

That was the freedom he was looking for. Back in Egypt, the government's censorship had abolished the freedom of the press and put a damper on the dissemination of ideas. He remembered the difficulty he faced in getting medical textbooks after Nasser had prevented the importation of foreign books. On a personal level, his indignation became more distressing when he remembered how that intolerant censorship had prevented Eva's letters from reaching him. *No wonder that Egypt had lost the Six-Day War,* he concluded.

A left turn took them to Forty Second Street and Times Square, where he was shocked to see, for the first time, the uncensored pornographic trade.

Eva reminded him of the ultimate expression of the freedom they were talking about—a pornographic district next to a public library.

When they reached the Hudson River Pier, the Circle Line ship was due to leave in thirty minutes.

"Good," she said. "This will give you enough time to try one of the traditional meals of New York."

She led him to the hot dog kiosk and ordered two hot dogs with sauerkraut, relish, and mustard, explaining that it was the American equivalent of the fool and falafel sandwiches of Cairo.

"What do you think?" She asked, after he had finished eating his.

"It is different, but it is equally messy, though not as filling. I think I need another one and a bottle of Coke to ease the burning in my stomach."

"Now you have become a true New Yorker."

She didn't have to explain anything during the cruise as the tour guide took over that duty. When the narration periodically stopped, they walked around the deck or stood on the bridge holding on to each other, as they sought to warm up themselves against the cool breeze of that autumnal day. When they reached the Statue of Liberty, he was overwhelmed by its size and exquisite details. He remembered the first time he heard about the Statue of Liberty, when his history teacher was talking about the construction of the Suez Canal. Somehow, he didn't feel sorry that Port Said had lost Lady Liberty to New York. That gigantic statue would have been out of proportion in the small square where the de Lesseps statue was. When he recalled that the de Lesseps statue was toppled after the 1956 War, he wondered if the same fate would have happened to Lady Liberty if her statue were the one that stood in that Egyptian square. He conceded that the New York Harbor, with its Liberty Island, had given Miss Liberty a more appropriate and a more permanent home.

"Eva," he said. "Did you know that this statue was originally offered to Egypt to stand at the entrance of the Canal in Port Said?"

"Yes, our school teacher was telling us the story of the building of the Suez Canal. Do you remember that school trip?"

"I have never forgotten any of the times I was with you, touched you, or even dreamed of you. You know that it was during that same trip that the idea of going to America first crossed my mind. It is funny that, to escape from Egypt, I thought at that time to work on one of those ships that crossed the canal. Here I am in America without the need to run away on a ship."

"I wonder what would have happened to us if we had stayed in Egypt. We weren't allowed to see each other, and certainly we would not have been able to get married. I would have died if that would have happened," she said.

He closed her mouth with his. Soon the tour guide resumed his narration, and they returned to their seats.

During the next intermission, he asked her about her mother. "Were you serious when you said in one of your letters that you hated your mother?"

"It's a long story," she started her explanation. "During our last year in Cairo, my mother seemed to be obsessed with the idea of finding a Jewish husband for me. She was afraid that I might fall in love with an Egyptian who might take me away from my Jewish heritage. I have to admit that her attitude made me consider running away from her and returning to my father. When we were about to leave Egypt, I had to make a choice. I could have ran away from my mother and stayed in Egypt, which meant that my father would regain custody over me, and he might pull me out of the university and force me to marry a Muslim man. Or I could get out of Egypt in the hope that I might end up in America where you would ultimately join me. My choice was easy; I left with my mother.

"We took a ship to Cyprus and from there to Israel. By the time I had finished college and started medical school, my mother was married to a wealthy Israeli. She was still obsessed with the idea of me getting married, even when we settled in Israel and there was no further threat of me marrying an Egyptian. We were fighting all the time. The thought of running away from my mother returned to me. Fortunately, my stepfather saved me from my predicament; he agreed to send me to America. Whether he did that through the goodness of his heart or just to get rid of me wasn't the issue. I didn't care anyway. I just wanted to get away from my mother."

"Did you see her after you have come to New York?"

"No. I didn't even see her when I went back during the war. I have a feeling she would have objected to our relationship; that's why I wouldn't tell her anything about us."

Their ship was cruising in the East River across from the financial center when Eva asked him about his parents.

"My father died last year from a heart attack. My mother developed a stroke just before I left Egypt," he told her. "My leaving wasn't easy for her, but she was very understanding. I really don't know if she will survive my departure."

"I am sorry to hear that."

"It's OK. All of us are destined to go one day or another. Have you heard from your father?"

"No, but I still have good memories of him. You remember how he was against my education and how he wanted me to get married? Well, that changed. I still believe that he was a good man. Why my mother took a stand against the Egyptians, being herself married to this good Egyptian, is beyond my comprehension."

The ship was approaching the three bridges of lower Manhattan, and the tour guide was narrating their histories. He then pointed to the important buildings on each side of the river: the Brooklyn waterfront and the Queens industrial area to the right, the United Nations building, the New York Hospital complex, the New York/Cornell Medical Center, and some of the waterfront apartments owned by or associated with famous people on the left. They listened attentively to the explanations, and gradually their remembrances retired to a subconscious level. It was after passing Upper Manhattan that David started to shiver from the cold weather on the exposed upper deck. With teary eyes and running nose, he followed Eva down the narrow steps to the enclosed lower deck. Eva sat him in a warm corner, went to the cafeteria, and came back with two cups of hot coffee. They stayed there for the remainder of their tour.

"Thank you, Eva," David said as they stepped out of the ship. "You let me see New York in one day."

"You ain't seen anything yet, as they say in New York. We have only scratched the surface. I have to show you, though, one more thing today."

They walked to Times Square where they descended into a subway station. "This is what I want you to see," she said. "Starting on Monday, you'll have to travel in the city by yourself. The subway is the best way to go to anywhere in the city."

She took a subway map and showed him how to use it. He was astonished at the extensive, underground subway grid.

"Where is the fifth borough on this map?" He asked when he recognized only four boroughs. She explained how Staten Island was connected to the rest of the city, not by the subway, but by a long suspended bridge and a ferry service.

"We'll take the subway back to our home," she said.

She bought two tokens and guided him through the turnstile. Sitting next to him in the subway car with the map spread on her lap, she resumed her lesson on how to navigate in the underground maze, pointing to the stations he should reach to access the important landmarks of New York. She circled the area of Central Park, the Metropolitan Museum of Arts, the Guggenheim Museum, and the Natural History Museum, emphasizing that he should visit them on his own when she returned to her work in the following week.

Out of the subway, she led him to a supermarket. She walked with him in every aisle, making sure to show him everything an American supermarket might display. He was astounded by the abundance of the items in front of him—nothing like the meager supplies in the Egyptian grocery stores. He couldn't help but remind her of the irony in the Egyptian saying, "Egypt is the mother of the whole world." In turn, she reminded him of the other ironic saying about the land that flows with milk and honey. They agreed that they were lucky to be in America, the true mother of the whole world and the land that actually flows with milk and honey.

Back in the apartment, he immediately dropped on the easy chair from utter exhaustion; the jet lag was evidently catching up with him.

"Don't you worry," she said. "I'll empty the shopping bags by myself. I don't need your help. You just take a nap until I prepare our dinner. Put on your pajamas and enjoy your sleep." She led him to the bedroom like a devoted and loving mother. "I'll be here when you wake up." She kissed him and left the room.

He didn't wake up until the next day. When he stretched his arm to search for her, he didn't find her. He raised his head to look around, but the early morning light was still too dim. He thought he was dreaming. He opened his eyes wide and gradually started to recognize his surroundings. He jumped out of bed and ran to the living room. His anxiety disappeared when he saw her sitting in her easy chair, reading a newspaper.

"Eva," he said. "You left me asleep all night."

She folded the newspaper and stood up to face him as he approached her. Seeing her in a nightgown for the first time brought a different and a new sentiment to his feelings.

"Eva," he repeated her name without waiting for her explanation. "I had an epiphany just now. When I saw you in the nightgown, I knew that we were husband and wife."

"You idiot, it took you that long to know what I have believed in since I got out of Egypt? I knew all along that you have always been a husband to me. That's why I didn't get married."

"Let's then make our marriage official," he said.

"I don't need a piece of paper to sanctify our marriage," she said.

"I don't need that either," he said. "What I mean is to take you to bed."

"I would love that," she said.

They stayed in bed, unable to move and unwilling to return from their transcendent trance, until the wailing of a speeding ambulance brought them back to reality. Gradually, the audible pulse of the city made them aware of space and time. A shared shower completed their transformation.

"I have a surprise for you," she said as she started to prepare the breakfast. "We are going to Carnegie Hall. Isaac Stern is playing Beethoven's violin concerto this evening."

She went to the bookshelf and inserted an LP on the record player. "This is a recording of the same concerto by David Oistrach. Let's listen to it while we eat our breakfast."

They finished eating before the end of the first movement and then sat on the sofa, next to each other, listening to the rest of the concerto. As he had memorized every note of that concerto, it wasn't too difficult for him to point to each theme and to explain the music with as little interference as possible.

"Now I know," she said after the music had stopped, "why you love classical music so much. How did you learn all that?"

"Partly at the Italian Institute where I was studying the violin, but mostly through Dr. Hussein Fawzy," he said.

When she didn't recognize that name, he explained, "Dr. Fawzy is a marine biologist and a music scholar. He has a weekly program on an Egyptian radio station dedicated to classical music. He is one of the very few people in the world who, not only understands classical music, but can also explain it clearly to the average listener. The only one who can come close to him is an American with the name of Carl Haas. He has a similar program on the BBC."

"I know him," she beamed with excitement. "He does have a weekly program on WQXR, which is the classical music station of the *New York Times*, our daily newspaper."

She showed him the newspaper she had been reading before he woke up. The *Times* was a surprisingly thick paper compared to the slim Egyptian dailies he was used to. She showed him that day's program of the classical music radio stations in the entertainment section of the paper, with all the listings of what was happening in the city.

"Eva," he said, after he had a quick look at the different headlines. "The choices are mind boggling. How can anyone choose from all of that?"

"You just have to get used to this abundance," she said with a big smile. "Wait until you shop for a car or even for food. You have already seen the tremendous choices in the supermarket. You might be tempted to call it the decadence of the capitalist culture, but you don't have to be part of it. You learn how to limit your choices. I made mine already. I don't have a TV. I subscribe to only one newspaper. I select my entertainment carefully. You have seen how fast I do my shopping. As the New York Times likes to say, 'You don't have to read it all, but it is nice to know that it's all there.' Similarly, you don't have to see it all, hear it all, or eat it all."

"I see your point," he said. Something else became clear in his mind. "Let me start with one pressing choice," he said. "Let's make our marriage official."

"Oh, what a backward person you are! But you have to tell me first, where we should get married, in a church or a mosque or a synagogue? You see. We do have to make a choice."

"None of the above," he said without hesitation.

"How about a civil marriage?" she asked.

"What? I thought you still believe in religion, or at least in the paranormal."

"Not anymore. You can call me an agnostic."

"Nonsense, you are not courageous enough to take a stand. Either you believe or you don't."

"I don't. How about you?"

"I am a confirmed atheist."

"How can you know with this certainty?"

"Eva, I have studied the three known religions. I have also studied the teachings of the oriental religions, if we might label them as such. They all have one common source, ignorance. On the other hand, science showed me the errors of the philosophical conclusions of the ignorant mind."

"Still, don't you agree that science does not give all the answers?"

"Of course, but this doesn't mean that religions give the definitive answer. Actually, the myths of God, Creation, and the afterlife were formulated by the primitive mind, remember ignorance, much earlier than when the relatively recent religions adopted and expanded on those myths."

Their discussion continued as such, until the light of the short autumnal day dimmed into an early darkness.

"Oh, my God," she screamed as she became aware of the late hour. "It is getting late. Let's grab a bite and head to Carnegie Hall. I can't wait to listen to this concerto live, now that you have explained it to me."

They had to stop their argument and prepare themselves for the concert. At any event, a conclusion on religion wasn't meant to be reached, and the decision on marriage didn't have to be made on that day.

To David's eyes, Carnegie Hall didn't look as lush and luxurious as the Cairo Opera House, where he had attended performances by La Scala of Milan, ballets by the Bolshoi and concerts by the various European orchestras. But seeing Isaac Stern, in person, was something else. Somehow, the glitter of New York, or the presence of Eva next to him, or Beethoven's music, or Stern's virtuosity, or all of the above filled him with boundless ecstasy.

The music was still echoing in David's head when they left the concert hall and walked toward the subway station. Instinctively, he assumed the posture of a violin player, and started to hum the ascending scale of the first theme of the first movement of the concerto, as his fingers glided over an imaginary violin neck. His make-belief playing came to an end when Eva engaged his arms in a tight embrace and his mouth in a kiss.

"You see what the city can do to you?" She said after she had stepped back to look at him. "Now when you see people in the streets talking to themselves or gesticulating in imaginary acts, you would understand their apparent craziness. Oh, how I love this city."

The spell of the music remained with them until they ended in bed and fell under the spell of a different kind. And the introduction to New York and to each other came to a happy conclusion. Reality caught up with them the next day.

MARRIAGE MADE IN HEAVEN

Before Eva left for work next morning, she gave David the application for the ECFMG and a copy of *Cecil-Loeb Textbook of Medicine.*

"You did bring your medical school documents, didn't you?" She asked as she handed him the application. He nodded. "You should send the completed application by registered mail. The main post office is at the corner of 34th Street and Eighth Avenue."

He took the directions, and then he questioned her about the textbook.

"Why do I need a textbook on internal medicine? He asked. "You know that I am a surgeon."

"Of course I know that," she said. "The ECFMG exam is mostly on general medical knowledge. You have been out of medical school for many years, and most likely you have forgotten the basic stuff. This book will refresh your memory and prepare you better for this exam."

He walked the streets of New York for the first time by himself. Without the comforting presence of Eva, he saw the tall buildings, the wide streets, and the long avenues in a different perspective, and a strange feeling of insignificance overwhelmed him. The oversized skyscrapers, and even the people of the city, reflected a sense of robotic grandiosity and overwhelming detraction from the elementary human dimension. What a tremendous contrast to his familiar and manageable Cairo. The cold windy weather of that November day didn't help, especially after the tips of his nose and ears froze, and a chilly sensation spread throughout his body. Not until he bought a hat and gloves did he dare to continue his walk to the post office. Alone, cold, and helpless, he didn't want to venture again into the threatening streets of the city. He mailed the application, walked a block to the closest subway station, and took the train back to the apartment.

He remembered where to find the classical music station—96.3 on the FM dial. He sat at the dining table and opened *Cecil-Loeb*, but he couldn't concentrate on reading, as the music that came from the stereo demanded his full attention. He should have known—listening to music and reading at the same time were incompatible, as if he were simultaneously sleeping with two women. He closed the book and listened to what he recognized as Mozart's music, the characteristically simple and logical notes. He thought of the flute concerto, but he quickly realized that that wasn't what he was listening to. Still, the melodies were somehow similar, and the structure was identical. He closed his eyes and listened until a clarinet took over; then it became clear to him that he was listening to a clarinet concerto by Mozart that he had never heard in his life. As the music faded away, the voice of the announcer confirmed the identity of the piece and its composer. How could he have missed this concerto before? But he had missed many other things as well. Now that he had all the choices in the world, it would be easier for him to canvas the rich musical repertoire. He decided to start his own musical library.

He was still listening to WQXR when Eva returned from her work.

"David," she said, after giving him a hug and a kiss, "I have found a job for you. There is a small hospital on 15th Street that needs house staff badly. They agreed to hire you without the ECFMG. You have to swallow your pride and work at the lowest level of the medical ladder. But remember, this is only a temporary job. Once you pass the ECFMG and with your qualifications, you will be able to get a residency in the best surgical programs in the country."

He followed her to the kitchen, where she started to prepare dinner as she continued her explanation. He would be called an extern, a non-accredited position, but with the duties of an intern. She gave him the name of the medical staff secretary and complete instructions on what was needed from him. With that settled, they sat down to eat.

As she was lighting the candles, he touched her hand and said, "Eva, we haven't reached a decision on our marriage yet."

"I thought we had settled this matter before," she said in a sarcastic voice. "I thought that we don't need a piece of paper to legitimize our relationship."

"We don't," he agreed. "However, a piece of paper would be desirable if we decided to have children. It would be unfair for them to be illegitimate."

"Who's thinking of children right now?" She asked.

"I am," he said. "Don't forget that both of us are over thirty now. It is not a good idea to have children at an older age."

"I know," she said. "But we don't have to be married to have children. In my opinion, our love has endured through space and time and insurmountable obstacles. This, and not a piece of paper, is what legitimizes our relationship and will surely make us better parents. However, I have no objection to a civil marriage, if that's what you want."

A civil marriage was agreed upon. He would get the license from the city hall, and she would arrange for the required blood test and the two witnesses. They might be able to finish all of that before he started his new job.

The next day, he submitted his credentials at the 15th Street hospital, obtained a marriage license from city hall, and finally ventured into the streets of the downtown area.

This time around, properly dressed for the cold weather and armed with a new, optimistic outlook, he saw the city in a different light. China Town and Little Italy, with their winding narrow streets, small shops, and aromas of ethnic food, reminded him of Cairo. He felt at home for the first time in New York, especially when he saw the obvious racial mix in that area. With a new sense of comfort and daring, he took the uptown subway, heading to the Metropolitan Museum of Arts.

The quantity and quality of the visual art he saw overwhelmed him. He remembered the motto of the *Times*, "You don't have to read it (or see it) all, but it is nice to know that it's all there." He made sure to scan the impressionist section, leaving the detailed study for later, when Eva would be with him. He spent the rest of that day in the Egyptian wing, where he was amazed by the wealth of the collection and the way every piece was artfully displayed. He knew that what was in front of him didn't compare to the immense collection at the Cairo Museum of Antiquities. But he had to admit that the Metropolitan not only preserved each piece well, but also exhibited his country's treasures in the most appealing and deserving fashion—without the cluttering, dust, and neglect he saw in Cairo museum. He sincerely wished that the Egyptian monuments received the same treatment in their original home in Egypt.

When Eva returned home, he gave her a full report on his accomplishments on that day. He expanded on what he saw in the museum, voicing his thoughts in more detail. His enthusiasm was infectious, and she promised to see the museum with him in the future. He spent the following days in the apartment, studying for the exam. Sure enough, he got the extern job, and the results of the blood test came back negative for syphilis. The marriage had to be finalized quickly. With the license in their hands, they took their two witnesses and appeared before a judge at City Hall. Finally, their marriage was legally certified.

The honeymoon was limited to the following two days of the weekend. Together, they sampled as much of the cultural life of the city as time allowed. They went to the Metropolitan and saw the impressionists' masterpieces together. When Eva listened to his description of every piece they looked at, she voiced her astonishment at his knowledge and understanding of modern art. But when she asked about the source of his information, he refrained from giving Magda the credit. After lunch in the museum's cafeteria, they spent the rest of their tour in the Egyptian section and recounted their shared memories in the old country. The next day they went to a matinee on Broadway and saw *Fiddler on the Roof*. They related to the music and the Jewish traditions of the *Fiddler*, as they saw in them aspects of their own heritage. They walked the

streets of Greenwich Village and ate falafel sandwiches at a Middle Eastern res-
taurant on 3rd Street. By the end of the two days, they had carried to the apartment, among other things, a large book on Claude Monet, *The Globe Illustrated
Shakespeare: The Complete Works,* a sizable number of classical music LPs, and
a violin. Their appetite for art and knowledge was voracious, and they started
quickly on their feast. When they ultimately settled in bed, they were the happiest couple in the world.

His job, even as an extern, proved to be very profitable; it introduced him
to the technologically driven American medicine. With this exposure, and
with the help of *Cecil-Loeb,* he passed the ECFMG exam without difficulty.
Subsequently, he was accepted as a first year surgical resident at the New York
University Hospital.

One evening, when they were reading *The Merchant of Venice* together, Eva
stopped at the scene where Shylock was justifying his thrifty behavior by quot-
ing the story of Jacob and Laban.

"Remember what you told me back in Cairo?" She asked. When David
looked at her in bewilderment, she said: "You told me then to read the Bible.
Well, I did."

"And?"

"This story as I read it in the Bible threw me off the same way it did when
I read *The Merchant* the first time. This particular story makes me question the
validity of all the religious tales."

"How is that?"

"There is no way that Jacob could have induced the goats to produce speck-
led and spotted offsprings by merely exposing them to the white streaks of the
green poplar and the chestnut trees. We know that genes control the hereditary
characteristics, not outside factors. This story, in particular, made me reread
the Bible in a more critical way."

They agreed that the stories of the Bible, as literarily fascinating as they
were, did not represent the historical truth. Everything in the Bible became
suspect, especially the story of the Creation. Growing up in the Middle
East, they were armed with intimate knowledge of the ancient Egyptian and

Mesopotamian civilizations. They couldn't help but see the confluence of ideas and the evolution of biblical thought from the accumulated myths of the area. They saw monotheism as an offshoot of the teachings of the philosopher, Pharaoh Akhenaton, who was the first in human history to think of one God. They recalled that even the Egyptian pantheon of gods, before Akhenaton, was derived from one supreme god, Ra. His descendants diverged to represent the good, in the person of Osiris, and the evil, in the person of his brother, Jeb. They knew how the myth unfolded to make Osiris marry his sister Isis and beget their son Horus—something like the holy trinity. They saw how the idea of death and resurrection was exemplified when Jeb ultimately killed his brother, Osiris, and the sister-wife Isis succeeded in collecting his scattered parts and returned him to life. At the end of the story, good ultimately triumphed against evil with human sacrifice and the spilling of blood, as the son Horus avenged his father and killed his uncle. They wondered at the recurrent theme in all mythology where good and evil and punishment and reward were always associated with sacrificial offerings and spilling of blood. Their inquiries extended to include more books and more research. David had already bought the nine volumes of Will Durant's *The Story of Civilization*. He opened the chapter on the story of the Creation as told in the much older Mesopotamian myth, which said, "In the beginning was Chaos, represented by the goddess Tiamat who created an emerging order out of the original Chaos and then destroyed it." As David was familiar with this myth, he explained to Eva the rest of the story and pointed to its similarity to the biblical narrative, including the flood that killed everyone except for a man and a woman who survived to restart the human lineage; the ritual of sacrifice to avoid further wrath from the gods; the tree of immortality and the serpent that stole it, depriving man of the desired immortality; and all those biblical incidents that were already told in the legend of Gilgamesh. For that matter, David recounted to her what he knew about the Mayan civilization in Central America. He concluded that other people who had inhabited far-away lands, distant from the lands that had produced the Bible and the Koran, had developed the same mythical narrative. And to their credit, they didn't claim a divine creator as a source of their inspiration.

"You know, Eva," David said one day, as if he was thinking aloud. "The Bible started to be written around 900 BC, and it was finally collected as a tome in the fifth century BC, after the Jews had returned from their exile in Babylon and much later than the alleged Exodus from Egypt, let alone the Creation itself. A history written thousands of years after the fact is an adulterated history. Oral transmission of stories, generations after countless generations, doesn't reflect the original truth of these stories. Besides, it is very clear to me that everybody at the time was influenced by everybody else—local mythologies were incorporated in other neighboring mythologies until the ultimate myth emerged."

"I agree," Eva said. "Still, for me these myths are as wonderfully human as the works of, say, Shakespeare. If a divine revelation was not the source of religion, and that imaginative and smart people had indeed written the holy books, there must have been a genuine need in human nature to explain the unknown, even if this explanation does not agree with the scientific facts. Despite my better judgment, I am not ready to renounce religion outright. This is not because I believe in the truths of religion, but because the scientific truths only reveal part of the whole picture. I have to stop at the limits of what science is telling me for certain and not declare a final verdict either way. I can only say that 'I don't know.'"

"Fair enough," he said. "Let's find out if the events told in the Bible actually occurred. Let's use the scientific laws and the documented historical records to verify the validity of the biblical story of the Creation, whether we take it literally or metaphorically and whether it is original or derived from primitive myths. The law of conservation of matter and energy won't allow for creating something out of nothing. Even if we allow for an omnipotent god who can create something from nothing, the cause and effect logic would lead us to an endless infinity. We have to ask who created this god to begin with, not withstanding the first unmoved mover of Aristotle. Even if that is permitted, the book of Genesis makes it impossible to reconcile the narrated events with the scientific facts. As calculated from the Bible, the history of the world wouldn't exceed ten thousand years or thereabout, which is contradicted by our geological, archeological, and paleontological findings. The idea of created species as final and perfect beings from the beginning does not reconcile with the tremendous varieties of the known species, let alone the Darwinian evolutionary theory, especially since we now have overwhelming evidence of its validity from new fossil finds and from the advanced genetic, molecular, and cellular-biological sciences. Adam and Eve, even if they had really existed, must have been the product of an evolutionary process that took billions of years; they did not appear instantly by the will of an omnipotent creator."

"I am not disputing your conclusions, but you have to agree that religions helped organize human societies and established the foundation for a moral behavior."

"I don't see it this way. Human societies evolved from the instinct for survival, and religious societies have no monopoly on human organization and morality. People who didn't have the benefit of revelation achieved similar standards of ethics and organizational systems. Actually, this same Jacob story reveals unethical behavior from Jacob and God. His behavior was outright cheating."

Eva persisted in her challenging mode. "But these stories and the codes of behavior that were derived from them formed the foundation of our modern civilization," she said. "In contrast, pagan societies, without guidance from moral dictates, deteriorated into ignorance, stagnation, and degeneration."

David accepted the challenge and answered her back. "What moral codes do you take from the Bible? Is it moral to select one group of people and condemn the rest to eternal hell, even if the chosen people proved to be disobedient and immoral? What morality is there in the Bible when a holy king sends a man to his assured death just to keep his wife for himself? What morality is there when killings and brutality are sanctified and incest is condoned? From the beginning of creation, the sons of Adam and Eve must have slept with their sisters to start the human line, which was inevitable and necessary. But when the daughters of Lot slept with their father, though the human race was not in danger of extinction, we have to question this morality. The pharaohs didn't think of morality when sisters and brothers married each other. Nature and necessity dictated their behavior, not false morality. I personally believe that ethics, in any event, are relative issues, changeable according to the dictates of the time and the demands for survival. But when Reuben, the first son of Jacob, slept with his stepmother, not out of necessity but out of lust, we can't put religion on a higher moral ground than that of the pharaohs. You see, Eva, your Jewish chosen people indulged in the same behavior, as did my un-chosen ancestral pharaohs, but the Exodus elevates one people over the other.

"Here, too, you have an unbelievable story. How can we believe the story of the Exodus with its dramatic catastrophic events, when these events were never mentioned in the records of the pharaohs, despite the fact that the pharaohs had recorded everything, even their most mundane daily activities, on stone or on durable paper in indelible ink? The plagues, the blood, and the parting of the waters of the Red Sea never happened; natural laws wouldn't allow such things. The killing of all first-born Egyptian children and the appropriation of the Egyptian jewels and treasures makes the chosen people, and God, far less moral than the Egyptians who saved Jacob and his descendants from starvation."

David and Eva, despite their atheistic conclusions, agreed on the literary beauty of the Bible and the Koran and judged them to be equal to the linguistic and dramatic mastery of the accumulated human literature. No miracles happened, but only the obvious talent of a genius mind, the same kind of genius mind that was equally apparent in the epics of Gilgamesh, *The Iliad, The Odyssey,* and in the music of Mozart and Beethoven.

···

Early in June, everything appeared to be falling in its proper place. Eva was three months into her pregnancy. She was finishing the second year of her residency in internal medicine and expecting to join a busy medical practice while remaining on the staff of the hospital after the end of her residency, a year later. David was soon to start his surgical residency at the New York University Hospital. In their spare time, he was practicing the violin, and she was sewing clothes for the soon-to-be-born baby. Together, they were reading Shakespeare, the Bible, and the Koran, and they considered themselves to be the happiest couple in the world. With a baby coming soon, and with two incomes to afford a bigger place, they were wait-listed for a two-bedroom apartment in the same building with the promise they would get it by July 1, the beginning of the new medical academic year. Alone, and without an extended family to celebrate their first Thanksgiving together, they ate the traditional festive meal as if they were sharing it with the whole world. When they felt a need to thank someone, they found only the gods of their own creation to thank. And they said a silent prayer to no one in particular.

TEL AVIV

E va delivered a healthy boy in December. From a long list of names, they ultimately settled on Adam.

"This time around, Adam must do a better job," David declared sarcastically.

As they watched Adam grow up, they celebrated each milestone of his development as if he were a genius and recorded all of them in countless photographs. They played music and read children's books to him. They talked with him in the two languages they knew. They planned his future that he might live their own unfulfilled dreams and carry their genes into a new family tree in their adopted country.

One day, when Adam was six months old, Eva returned from her work with a letter in her hand.

"David," she said, "I have to go to Israel."

This unexpected statement took David by surprise. He glanced at the envelope and recognized an Israeli postage with the Star of David on it.

"Anything happened to your mother?" He asked.

"Not yet," she said, as she handed him the letter. "Actually, the letter is from my mother. Why don't you read it yourself?"

The letter was written in the Arabic language. After a moment of surprise, he realized that it was logical that Eva's mother would write in Arabic; she never had the necessary education to write in English or Hebrew.

He started to read: "I am dying from metastatic breast cancer. As I approach inevitable death, I have to unload the secret of my life. What I have to tell you, I can't write in a letter. I have to tell it to you personally, face to face. Come to your mother as soon as you read this letter or else you will never see me alive again. My secret has everything to do with you, so please come as soon as you can…"

"What does this mean?" David said without reading the rest of the letter. "Eva, you must have an idea about this secret, don't you?"

"Yes and no," she answered in a hesitant voice. "I don't know where to start. It's a long story. Let me first call the airline to book my flight, and then I'll tell you the part of this secret that I am aware of."

She called the El Al office and booked a flight to Tel Aviv for the following Monday. She then turned to David and said: "There are only two more weeks left in my residency, and I am sure that they don't mind me leaving now; there isn't much work to be done anyway. You know what it is like at the end of any residency program."

He wasn't interested in the residency program. All he wanted to know was that secret. A premonition gave him a sinking feeling that was justified by the revelation that soon followed.

"I always had a lingering suspicion that my mother was cheating on my father," she started her story.

Her doubts started to torment her at the time of her parents' divorce, not that they had told her anything, but by a mere coincidence when she overheard them argue during the days leading to the divorce. Her father was accusing her mother of adultery; he called her a whore. When Eva confronted her mother after the divorce, her mother dismissed it as nothing of consequence. "Your father is a jealous man," she said. "He frequently accuses me of adultery. We divorced because I couldn't take it anymore. Divorces happen all the time. There is nothing unusual about that." Her mother repeated the same story whenever the subject was brought up.

Ultimately, Eva had to accept her mother's explanation, although she deeply believed that her mother was cheating on her husband. This uncertainty so overwhelmed her that she was about to run away, except for the reality of the Egyptian culture and a genuine fear of being on her own. The divorce lessened her torment but not her doubts. Still, some unanswerable questions remained in her mind.

"How come he allowed you to take me away from him?" She had questioned her mother on one occasion.

"You were at the university in Cairo," her mother had told her. "Your education was our primary concern. I happened to have the help of a wealthy Jewish family, which would have made your life a lot easier if you came with me. Your father saw the advantage of that arrangement, and he accepted it for your own sake."

Eva reasoned that her mother's explanations didn't make sense. She knew that a Muslim father would insist on raising his daughter as a Muslim. Why did he give up on that religious and cultural duty? She frequently asked, but her mother did not deviate from telling the same story and the same explanation. Once they settled in Israel, which gave Eva a new identity and her mother's maiden name, her pressing need to believe in the virtue of her mother relegated her doubts to a safe repository in her mind.

"I am scared," Eva said when she had finished. "However, whatever the secret is, even if my mother is an adulteress, I have to live with it. But, you have to assure me that my mother's character won't interfere with our relationship."

"How could you ever say a thing like that?" David asked as a jolt of incredulity shook him. "I fell in love with you because of who you are, not because of your mother or father."

"But when it comes to marriage and children and genetics, you never know, especially with how we were brought up."

"I don't believe what you have just said. I love your mother because she brought you to this world. Her character will never be an issue with me. I will continue to love you no matter what the secret turns out to be."

"Don't be upset. I just wanted to be reassured."

There was only one way to reassure her. He held her in his arms and carried her to bed, and the fears faded away as they became one in body and soul. Monday afternoon Eva took an El Al flight to Tel Aviv.

An emaciated semblance of the mother she had known opened the door when Eva rang the bell. It took Eva a mere glance to realize the terminal stages of cancer in her mother's figure. The fingerprints of chemotherapy—from sunken cheeks, bruised skin, and hair loss—were obvious. A sinking feeling overwhelmed Eva, and a filial compassion banished all the long-held animosity she held toward her mother. She embraced her tenderly and led her to bed.

When she looked around and didn't find anybody else in the apartment, Eva asked her, "Where is your husband?"

"He left me after I had lost my breast to surgery," her mother said. "Heaven has been punishing me for my sins. You left me, two husbands left me, and now I am suffering from this cancer and about to die alone."

"Don't say that," Eva said. "I am here now, and I'll help you."

"Nobody can help me. Eva, don't feel sorry for me. I deserve all the suffering I have been going through. Somehow, I couldn't die until I had seen you. I knew that you would come. My daughter, I am not dying from cancer, although it has spread all over," her mother said and paused to catch her breath. "I am dying nevertheless but from something else that is not killing my body but my soul." Her breathing became shallow and labored. Her face contorted from apparent pain.

"Mother, you are in pain," Eva became frightened. "Don't they give you something for these pains?"

"They do." She couldn't talk except in short sentences. "I skipped...the... last dose...this drug...makes me...drowsy. I didn't want...to be...drowsy... for you." She stopped for a moment to catch her breath and to regain enough strength to explode her bomb in one uninterrupted sentence. "Eva, your father is not your real father."

Eva didn't remember what happened next. All she recalled was that, somehow, she found herself in the arms of her mother. They didn't exchange any more words for the rest of the day, as if they were drained by the revelation. It took her mother an eternity to tell the whole story, as her pains and difficult breathing made her talk in short and, sometime, incoherent sentences.

Her mother fell in love with Mohammad and married him over the objections of her family. Her family subsequently ostracized her, but one brother finally relented and kept in touch with her. He was the uncle who helped her with the divorce and got her the legal custody of Eva.

Although Mohammad was a good husband, he was a deeply jealous one, especially because he was on the road most of the time. She didn't mean to cheat on him, but one day when he was away, she fell ill. A neighboring friend nursed her during her illness. When she got better, the neighbor continued to look after her needs. One day, they were alone in the house talking and enjoying a cup of coffee together. She didn't know what happened, but it did happen. They went to bed only that one time, and that time was all it took. Eva was the product of that encounter.

At this part of the story, the mother lapsed into sleep. Eva was about to faint from fear and anticipation. However, she managed to keep her strength to shake her mother out of her sleep.

"Mother," Eva screamed, unable to hide her anxiety. "Who was that neighbor?"

"Bishara."

That's all that Eva heard before she collapsed on the floor. When she regained her consciousness, she was too dazed to comprehend what it all meant. Straightening herself, she saw a bewildered expression covering her mother's face.

"Did you mean that Mr. Bishara is my real father?" Eva asked. Her mother could only nod.

Eva started to convulse spasmodically, as if an evil spirit had overtaken her body. She walked around the room. She cried, and she laughed hysterically. It took her a few minutes to comprehend the enormity of that revelation. She approached the bed like a robot, held her mother by the shoulders, and shook her as she screamed hysterically.

"Do you realize what you have done to me?" Eva finally asked. She hesitated for only a moment, as if to gather enough strength to hit her mother with a blow strong enough to let her feel all the torment she felt in her heart.

"Mother!" Eva shouted from the depth of her lungs. "I am married to David, Mr. Bishara's son."

It was her mother's turn to collapse. Eva kept on repeating the same sentence and shaking her mother incessantly, as if to keep her awake to suffer the pain her sentence must have inflicted on her.

"You have married your brother." That's all her mother could say before she fell into a coma.

Eva went to the hospital every day with the hope of finding her mother awake enough to explain the missing links in her story. This happened during the few moments of consciousness that her mother experienced before she died.

Eva's mother was confident that Bishara was Eva's father as Mohammad was away at that time. To leave no doubt about that fact, she mentioned that Mohammad was sterile; she couldn't get pregnant by him despite many years of trying. "He was simply infertile," she declared.

But the poor man believed that he had induced her pregnancy, and she didn't want to devastate him by the truth or ruin her life by a secret that nobody was privy to anyway. Even Mr. Bishara didn't know the truth. How could he when he had slept only one time with a married woman, who could have naturally conceived through her own husband?

She loved her daughter so much that she didn't dare to let anyone know of her illegitimate conception, even if she had to keep her own daughter in the dark. She never thought of David as more than a neighbor and a schoolmate. It was inconceivable in the Egyptian society that a boy would fall in love with, let alone marry, a girl from a different religion.

"Eva, you hated me when I tried to get you married to a Jewish boy, a relative of ours. You hated me when I took you out of Egypt," she said at one point. "Now I know why."

Eva's mother said that once they had reached Israel, she figured out that Eva had become safe from all Egyptian men, Christians and Muslims alike. However, it was already too late to regain her daughter's friendship. What she most certainly cared about was that Eva was safe, and there was no need for anyone to know her true identity. The truth became an albatross to be carried by the mother alone. Nobody else should suffer from its weight or its consequences, especially Eva.

"I am deeply sorry, Eva," Eva's mother said when she had finished. "I am the one who sinned, but you are the one to bear the punishment."

As if she was resisting death just to finish her story, she exhaled her last breath once she uttered the last sentence.

Overwhelmed by the facts, Eva couldn't decide what should be her next move. Thankfully, the funeral arrangements distracted her from her own thoughts. She remained numb, as if in a trance, until she had buried her mother and found herself on a flight to New York.

During the twelve-hour flight, she stayed awake, victimized by her thoughts and tormented by the need for a decision. It was at Kennedy Airport, and only after she had seen Adam, that she reached her decision. When she hugged the baby, she felt strong enough to face her inevitable fate. Seeing the inquisitive expression on David's face, she didn't have to wait for his question. She had already made up her mind.

"David," she said. "My mother was a saint burdened by the degenerate Middle Eastern moral and religious inheritance. Adam shouldn't suffer from this culture that has demeaned the basic and inherent human needs. Let's go home."

...

ABOUT THE AUTHOR

Dr. **Fouad Bishay Michael** is a retired physician and writer living in Charlottesville, Virginia. After graduating from the Medical School of Cairo University in Egypt, he immigrated to the United States, where he did his postgraduate studies and became Board Certified in Otolaryngology-Head and Neck Surgery. He was the Chief of the Otolaryngology Department at Mercy Medical Center in Rockville Centre, New York, and a teacher in a residency program at the New York Eye and Ear Infirmary Hospital in Manhattan. In addition, he managed a private practice in Long Island, NY. He finally retired at the age 62 to devote his time to writing.

He studied creative writing, philosophy, biology, literature, and cosmology at Molloy College in Rockville Center, NY, and at the University of Virginia and its affiliates in Charlottesville, Virginia. He spends his time reading, writing, sculpting, listening to classical music, and playing the Flute.

Publications:
    Books:
    *In the Guts of Health care (Authorhouse, 2004)
    *Ingenious Nonsense (Authorhouse, 2012)
    *Egyptian Immigrants, a book of short stories, to be published soon.
    *Neo-Genesis, a parody, to be completed in the near future.
Essays:
    *Several essays on health care issues were published in medical journals and newsletters.
    *Several letters-to-the editor were published in daily newspapers.

CPSIA information can be obtained at www.ICGtesting.com
Printed in the USA
LVOW01s1944081013

356011LV00029B/1331/P